WILDERNESS WEEKENDS

WILD ADVENTURES IN BRITAIN'S RUGGED CORNERS

PHOEBE SMITH

First edition published March 2015
Bradt Travel Guides Ltd
IDC House, The Vale, Chalfont St Peter, Bucks SL9 9RZ, England
www.bradtguides.com
Print edition published in the USA by The Globe Pequot Press Inc,
PO Box 480, Guilford, Connecticut 06437-0480

Text copyright © 2015 Phoebe Smith
Maps copyright © 2015 Bradt Travel Guides Ltd Contains Ordnance Survey Data © Crown
copyright and database 2015
Photographs copyright © 2015 Individual photographers (see below)
Project Managers: Mike Unwin and Anna Moores
Cover design and research: Pepi Bluck, Perfect Picture
Design: Pepi Bluck, Perfect Picture

ISBN: 978 1 84162 912 4 (print)
e-ISBN: 978 1 78477 117 1 (e-pub)
e-ISBN: 978 1 78477 217 8 (mobi)

British Library Cataloguing in Publication Data
A catalogue record for this book is available from the British Library

Photographs
Front cover Top image: Wild camping above Loch an Dubh-Lochain; bottom image: View across
Rannoch Moor (Loop Images Ltd/A)
Back cover Waking up after a wild night on the Ardnamurchan Peninsula, Scotland
Title page Sneaking a bivvy bag sleep under Whitendale Hanging Stones, Lancashire
All photographs copyright © 2015 Phoebe Smith/Neil S Price, except for individual
photographers credited beside images and also those from picture libraries, credited as
follows:
Alamy (A); Dreamstime.com (D); www.flpa.co.uk (FLPA); Shutterstock.com (S).

Maps Pepi Bluck, Perfect Picture and David McCutcheon FBCart.S

Typeset from the author's disc by Pepi Bluck, Perfect Picture
Production managed by Jellyfish Print Solutions; printed in the UK
Digital conversion by www.dataworks.co.in

AUTHOR

Having grown up on the edge of Snowdonia National Park, in North Wales, Phoebe Smith's love of dramatic landscapes has taken her on walking and backpacking adventures all around the world – from wild camping on the Scottish islands and sleeping under a swag in the Australian outback to watching the Northern Lights from a wigwam above the Arctic Circle. She's enjoyed snowshoeing in the Swiss Alps, scrambling in Wadi Rum and canyon walking in the USA. But of all the places she's been, it's the UK that holds the  dearest place in her heart. She is adamant that you don't need to travel far to have an adventure and when not planning her next escapade she's most likely to be found in the mountains with her trusty tent.

Back in the office, Phoebe is editor of *Wanderlust* travel magazine – Consumer Magazine of the Year 2013 (PPA Independent Publisher's Awards) – and has written extensively for a range of newspapers and magazines both in the UK and overseas. Her other books include *Extreme Sleeps: Adventures of a Wild Camper*; *Wild Nights: Camping Britain's Extremes*; *The Camper's Friend*; *The Joy of Camping*; *Peddars Way and Norfolk Coast Path* and *Book of the Bothy*.

ACKNOWLEDGEMENTS

Special thanks to Neil for the beautiful photographs and unwavering enthusiasm for my work. And to my dad for never asking too many questions and always being there no matter what.

This book is dedicated to all those who will never find the time, money or courage to cross continents, row oceans or climb the highest mountains. You are about to find that adventure waits just around the corner.

WILDERNESS WEEKENDS

SCOTLAND

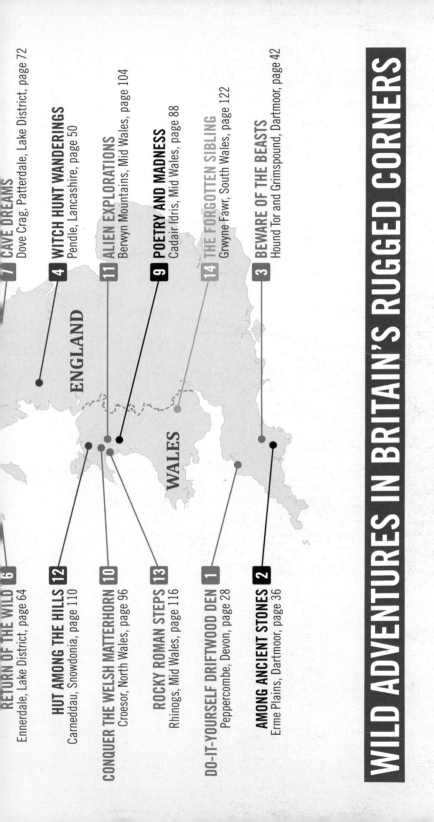

ENGLAND

WALES

WILD ADVENTURES IN BRITAIN'S RUGGED CORNERS

CONTENTS

INTRODUCTION

"AS YOU SIT ON THE HILLSIDE, OR LIE PRONE UNDER THE TREES OF THE FOREST, OR SPRAWL WET-LEGGED BY A MOUNTAIN STREAM, THE GREAT DOOR, THAT DOES NOT LOOK LIKE A DOOR, OPENS."

Stephen Graham, *The Gentle Art of Tramping*

Catching sight of my sunburnt face in the rear-view mirror of my car after my first solo wild camp in Wales, I knew something had changed. Covered in midge bites, my hair plastered to my forehead with sweat, I had never looked less glamorous. And yet, at the same time, I don't think I'd ever looked so good. I had just returned from a two-day expedition into the mountains, by myself, with nobody to rely upon, and had survived. The feeling of liberation – of knowing that this was something I could do – was almost indescribable. That I could go out into a wild place and return relatively unscathed made me feel the most confident I had ever felt. I knew then and there that the itch I now had to scratch went much deeper than the sunburn. Something in me had awoken: a desire to explore more of Britain's remote landscapes. I had become an instant addict.

Ever since that day, more years ago than I care to admit, I've made it my mission to seek out wildness in my home country. Before then I had spent the best part of two-and-a-half years travelling around the world, convinced that Adventure, with a capital 'A', lurked only in far-off lands – from the Red Centre of Australia and the high Arctic plains of Lapland to the mountainous spine of Nepal, the USA's largest national parks and the starry desert skies of Jordan. But since then I have proved to myself – and now aim to prove to you in this book – that you needn't travel far to have an adventure. Britain offers a wealth of opportunity to not only gaze upon some of the best scenery you'll find anywhere, but also to sleep in its wild embrace on your own mini-expedition.

In short, after a childhood spent not appreciating what lay waiting in my own backyard, I now revel in the adventures I can find in precisely that place. And I would like others to realise exactly the same. You see, I'm not your typical adventurer: I don't try to be a superhuman Bear Grylls-style survivalist; I haven't sailed around the world; I have no desire

to cross a continent on foot or by bike; and I cannot grow the obligatory expeditioner's beard. If I do have an extraordinary quality, it is that of being simply an ordinary person – in search of excitement and adventure – just like you – but without wanting all the expense and corporate sponsorship, or having to survive by feasting on a decaying sheep's carcass. I don't believe in conquering the elements or in fighting the epic battle between man and nature. My motto has always been 'enjoy, not endure'. And that's why I wrote this book: to show that everyone – you included – can go into the wildest places and survive.

After the 2013 publication of my book *Extreme Sleeps*, describing my journey from mattress lover to wild sleeper, I received hundreds of emails and Tweets asking for advice on exactly where to 'find Britain's wild spaces', how to pack and prepare for these adventures, and how safe I thought it was to attempt them. The internet is a fantastic place in which to seek information on, say, buying tents or sleeping bags, but visit a forum of outdoor folk and dare to ask for recommendations on a good wild camp spot, and you're liable to be met with people telling you you should already know your own – or even chastising you for having the audacity to ask.

There will be some, of course, who think I should not have shared these locations. But I truly believe that the more people who visit them and fall in love with them, as I have, the more eyes will be watching over them and protecting them. It dismays me to read that children these days spend significantly less time outdoors than their parents did. How can they learn to love and cherish something if they've never experienced it? I hope my words offer people the chance to do just that, and that future generations will work hard to protect these wild places for others to enjoy.

I'm not going to lie to you: getting into true wilderness is not always easy. But I can promise you that the pay-offs are worth the effort: from that first 'reveal' moment in the morning when, having arrived in near darkness the night before, you first spy how breath-taking your location is by daylight, to the satisfying feeling of knowing you are right in the thick of it while friends and family are still at home in bed. And once you feel that sense of achievement from surviving your first wild sleep, and experience that amazing high that comes when you return to your car or your home immediately afterwards, you will know – as I first did all those years ago – that things will never quite be the same again.

So, welcome to my world of wild nights out. It's cool to have you along for what I know will be an exciting journey. But enough talk. Just grab your Go Bag (see page 17), your OS map and your thirst for adventure, and together we will head into the wild.

Phoebe Smith
March 2015 ☉ www.phoebe-smith.com

WILDERNESS WEEKENDS: THE ESSENTIALS

Having the right kit will ensure that you remember your wilderness experience for all the right reasons, and not because you got damp and miserable in a leaky tent. People will tell you that you don't need to spend a fortune to wild camp or sleep in a cave – and of course that is true. But it pays to be well equipped. The trick with gear is always striking a balance between weight and comfort. In an ideal world, we'd all like the essentials to weigh virtually nothing but still keep us super warm and dry. Of course there are some über-featherweight items that do work amazingly efficiently, but you'll need a lot of cash for these. Bear in mind, also, that shaving off the grams will usually mean reducing at least some comfort. This leaves us with a two-part dilemma: first, what is the lightest affordable option; second, how much comfort will you forgo for the sake of lightness. So let's start with the essentials:

TENTS

Although the arrival of glamping has spawned all kinds of tents, for wilderness weekends you'll generally be looking at two types: Geodesic and Tunnel.

Geodesic tents are sometimes dome-shaped but, at the lighter end of the spectrum, more often like a pyramid. Either way, the key is that, with the poles in place, this is a freestanding structure. You can simply move it to the best place and peg it down. Geodesic tents offer the most stable designs and are the ones most used on high-altitude expeditions. They are also my personal favourites. The downside – unless you pay top dollar – is their weight.

Tunnel tents, by contrast, rely on you to create the final shape, using your excellent pegging skills. They come with fewer poles than geodesic tents – usually just two that bend over to create the trademark shape – so they are generally lighter. They also usually offer a little more headroom and so are good for sitting inside in a storm. The downside? You will need to create good tension when pegging out to get these working at their best

– ensuring, in particular, that the inner and outer sheets don't touch (this being the cause of the condensation that leads many people to thinking their tent is leaking). Also, the flatter roof shape can mean rain and snow will collect more easily in the middle and make it sag, again causing the problem above.

It all comes down to personal choice, of course. Before you buy, ask the shop whether you can try erecting the tent beforehand to see if it's right for you. Remember that pitching in calm, dry conditions is always very different from trying to put up your tent in a storm on the side of a mountain: if you can't do it in the shop, then you've no chance doing it outside.

Whatever the tent you choose, remember when packing that you don't have to keep it in the original bag. If there's more than one of you, split the weight: one person can take the sheets; another the poles and pegs. Also, try popping it into a dry bag, instead of the manufacturer-supplied one, as you'll normally manage to squeeze it down smaller.

BIVVY BAGS

Bivvy bags – also known as 'bivy' or 'bivi' bags, the word being short for 'bivouac' – are an increasingly popular option. They range from the insanely cheap to the insanely expensive, with those at the high end being better than some budget tents. A bivvy bag, in a nutshell, is a waterproof bag that slips over your sleeping bag, body bag-style, keeping you dry. That's the theory. The reality is that even in a good bivvy bag, with good breathability, your sleeping bag will still get damp due to condensation. This isn't a problem for one night, but bear in mind that in the rain it can become unbearable.

A good compromise is a hooped bivvy, which will not only keep the fabric off your face but also usually incorporates a mosquito net that keeps the midges at bay. Another, ever more popular option, is to use a combination of bivvy bag and tarp (tarpaulin): the latter is basically a sheet of fabric, which you pitch over your bivvy using walking poles or trees, and that keeps the rain off.

Again, it all comes down to personal choice. On a clear night, in dry conditions, on a mountain summit or inside a cave, a bivvy bag cannot be beaten. However, if the weather's looking iffy then stick to my motto – 'enjoy not endure' – and take a tent instead.

SLEEPING BAGS

Again, there's a huge choice when it comes to sleeping bags. Personally, I need to be warm to sleep well, and if I don't sleep well I won't be able to enjoy the next day so I am prepared to take a slightly heavier sleeping bag. As with a tent, a higher price will normally get you a better balance between weight and warmth, which really is the key. Check the temperature ratings on the bags, but remember these are not a science – the 'comfort' rating is the one to heed rather than the 'extreme'. Then think about yourself as an individual. Do you tend to sleep hot or cold? Would you happily endure a worse night's sleep in order to carry more weight in food? Do you want to use it year-round or realistically will you only do this in the summer? It's a very personal choice.

Sleeping bags will have two filling options: down or synthetic. Down, from a goose or duck, offers the best warmth-to-weight ratio and packs down the smallest. However, get a down bag wet and you'll know about it, as it stops the feathers lofting – that is trapping the warm air – so you'll get cold quickly. Synthetic performs much better when wet compared with down and can be a fair bit cheaper, but remember it will also often be a bit heavier.

Finally, don't forget that sleeping bags do come in gender-specific models – ie: for men and women. There's a good reason for this, as women tend to lose more heat through their feet and have wider hips, whereas men tend to have broader shoulders and need a more even spread of warmth. Manufacturers know this, so tailor bags accordingly. But it doesn't mean you have to go with the one made for your gender: shorter, wider men who get cold feet may find a women's version a better fit; for tall, broad women, it may be vice versa.

The main thing to remember when choosing your sleeping bag is to trust yourself. Don't opt for a model because your brother/best friend/that girl who wrote *Wilderness Weekends* likes it. Go with what's best for you.

SLEEPING MAT

This is another product that comes in a wide price spectrum. At the one end you have the simple roll-up foam offerings, which do definitely help remove some of the chill from the ground. You'll often find people leave these behind in caves and bothies, and you can even pick them up in a Pound shop. With higher prices the models become better cushioned and usually crush down smaller. And then there's the inflatable variety: for the most comfort and the best night's sleep, I have to recommend a Therm-a-rest NeoAir, which packs down to smaller than a beer can and weighs in at just 350g (that's regular size; smaller and larger options are available), so is friendly both underneath you and on your back.

CAMPING STOVE

For both heating up your evening meal and purifying water, this is a wild camping essential. There are several options, from alcohol-burning Trangias (once the favourite of Duke of Edinburgh groups), to Ray Mears-style Kelly Kettles that run on burning twigs and sticks, or the more efficient and quicker gas stoves. The first two are good for car camping or for entertaining kids looking for things to burn, but wilderness weekends require something that packs small and works so efficiently that you don't have to carry extra fuel. For that you'll want a gas stove. There are lots of small and easily packable ones on the market, but do remember you'll need a pan to use with them. An alternative and excellent option is the Jetboil, which not only burns gas and boils water efficiently in all weathers but is also a complete cup/jug combi. Just don't forget to take your spork (spoon, fork, knife combination).

FIRST AID KIT

It's important that you take the basics with you when going into the wild, but leave the all-singing, all-dancing kit at home. So what to put in it? Essentials are: any prescribed medication; blister plasters (Compeed are highly recommended); sterilised wipes (for cuts/grazes); plasters; a tick remover or pointed tipped tweezers; painkillers (eg: Paracetamol) and anti-inflammatories (eg: Ibruprofen); a small, basic penknife; and storm-proof matches. Finally, duct tape will not only fix torn tents and rucksack straps, but also tape up damaged fingers – and more. Again, tailor your kit for where you are going and how long you will be away. And make sure you know how to use everything in it.

13

ACCESSORIES AND EXTRAS

Other miscellaneous essentials include: a head torch (with spare batteries); a whistle; a warm hat (you may want to sleep in it); warm and waterproof gloves (plus a pair of thinner warm liner gloves to wear underneath in very cold weather or on their own when it's warmer but not wet); and a buff (keep it round your neck to keep you warm; also works as a headband, dust mask and even – in an emergency – a tourniquet). Also, I always pack a set of dry socks and underwear for bed, and bring along an inflatable pillow – my one little luxury. Don't forget your small toothbrush and toothpaste.

KEEPING EVERYTHING DRY

Rucksack covers certainly help, but water always gets in eventually. Another way is to line your rucksack with a large dry bag and then use smaller dry bags to compartmentalise your kit inside: one for bedtime items, one for food, one for accessories, etc. Failing that, the cheapest short-term option is a bin liner.

FOOD AND DRINK

I can't emphasise enough the importance of taking good food. Nothing can make a bad situation instantly better than a hot meal or drink. I know a girl who once made the mistake of taking a salad wild camping and spent a very miserable night in a wet tent never feeling warm.

For your main evening fare the best option is a pre-packed camping meal. Not only is this lightweight, but also packed with the calories and proteins your body will need after hauling your backpack around the wild. You have two choices: dehydrated (simply add boiled water and wait for it to cook in about ten minutes) or boil in the bag (takes around the same time). The latter is heavier but is pre-cooked so, if stuck without water, you could eat it cold.

For the rest of the time you want snacks – and lots of them. Think slow-burn calories, such as nuts, cereal/granola bars, dried fruit, plus some quick-release sugary treats like chocolate bars. No matter how many you think you'll need, always take more: the worst thing you can do is run out of food, especially in a scenario when you need to think straight. I always like to take a bag of sweets (eg: Jelly Babies, Haribos) for that point in the walk when I need an instant boost.

For drinks, water is best. Drink plenty of it. I tend to take hot chocolate sachets for before bed and all-in-one coffee sachets for the morning. There are some people who swear that they've drunk straight from fast-flowing streams and have always been fine. Best to ignore them: even if water looks clean you have no idea what's in it and it's never worth the risk. Always boil water or use sterilising tablets to make it safe to drink. Look for fast-flowing streams rather than still pools. Boiling is the easiest and most failsafe method of sterilisation. A good tip is to boil enough water in the evening to fill your water bottle then (taking care not to burn yourself) wrap the bottle in your fleece. You now have a perfect hot water bottle to keep you warm all night then, by morning, a supply of cool clean drinking water for your walk out. Genius!

CLOTHING

When heading into wild places you need to dress right to ensure you don't get too hot or too cold. The best way to do this is with a layering system: you wear a series of thinner layers, rather than one big warm one, so that you can add or remove one as conditions dictate. This consists of the following:

Baselayer

This is the clothing that sits right against your skin. Whether you prefer long or short sleeves, look for merino wool (best in winter) or synthetic fabrics that wick sweat away from your skin, keeping you cool and dry. Cotton is a bad idea.

Midlayer

This goes over the top of the baselayer and keeps you warm. You can buy a fancy 'softshell' to do this job but, to be honest, I find a fleece is still the best option: it's light, cheap and instantly warming. Microfleece is best of all, though costs a little more.

Outershell

This is your waterproof. Look for Gore-Tex, eVent or the equivalent: something that is highly breathable and waterproof and also helps keep the wind off.

The great thing about a layering system is that you don't have to wear all the layers at once. If it's windy or raining and not particularly cold you can wear the outershell over the baselayer and forget the midlayer. If it's cold but dry, simply wear the baselayer and midlayer and don't add the outer.

15

In winter, in the mountains or very cold weather (or if you really feel the cold), you should also consider taking an extra layer for insulation. This will be a jacket stuffed with down or synthetic fabric and big enough to go over all three layers at once. It's great for when you stop for lunch (a time when you will always lose heat), to read your map or once you've set up camp and are sitting still.

For the lower part of your body it's the same method: baselayer pants/ long johns for cold weather or to sleep in, a good softshell pair of walking trousers (look for breathable, water-resistant fabric that's robust but light, articulated knees for ease of movement and zippable pockets), then waterproof overtrousers for when it rains. And last, but not least, don't forget the importance of a good pair of socks. Look for those made for purpose: breathable, warm, seam-free and comfortable.

SHOES OR BOOTS?

There's a whole debate about whether walking is best done in traditional boots or shoes. As with most things in the outdoors, this is something best decided by you. The advantage of boots is that, reaching above your ankles, they can keep your feet drier – especially on boggy ground or when crossing small streams. They also offer ankle support on rocky and rough ground, which is especially useful when carrying a heavy rucksack. Shoes are usually a much lighter option, however, and if you've done a lot of walking on mixed terrain you may feel perfectly comfortable and confident just using them.

Or course, the choice is never quite that straightforward. Among boot models you can get very flexible or very stiff ones, just as you can with shoes. Flexible boots will be lighter and more comfortable in the short term but over long walks your feet will be working harder and are likely to become more tired. You will also be able to feel more through them on stony and rocky ground. Stiff boots will mainly be heavier and often uncomfortable on very flat, even sections but come into their own when edging along rocks or scrambling.

So, perhaps rather unhelpfully, there is no right answer. It's a case of trying what's right for you and your feet. Either way, no matter what you opt for, before heading out on your wilderness weekend do make sure you wear in your footwear first. You don't want to get any unexpected blisters in the first couple of hours that could ruin your experience.

INTRODUCING MY GO BAG

One tip I always offer those who want to explore the wild is to have what I call a 'Go Bag' ready packed at all times. It's basically a rucksack I keep, either next to my front door or in the boot of my car, filled with all the essentials I need for at least one night's wild camping. That way, if the mood takes me or the opportunity or weather window arises, I have no excuses. I'm ready for my wild weekend.

Choose a bag with a capacity of 40–50 litres. I use a women-specific pack but you should try on as many as possible – full – to find what sits best on your body shape. It should contain the following:

- Tent/bivvy
- Sleeping mat
- Sleeping bag
- Camping stove and pot/pan
- Gas
- Spork (spoon/knife/fork combination)
- Mug
- First-aid kit
- Head torch
- 'Bedtime dry bag' including: inflatable pillow, toothbrush and paste, dry socks, change of underwear, tissues, thermal base layer trousers
- 'Accessories dry bag', including warm gloves, hat and buff
- Fleece/midlayer top
- Waterproof jacket
- Insulated jacket
- Waterproof overtrousers
- Water bottle
- Food
- More food
- Walking poles

Optional (depending on time of year):
- Insect repellent
- Sunscreen

So what are you waiting for? Go and make yours up now before reading any further.

NAVIGATION

Heading into the wilder parts of Britain will require an ability to navigate, so you could argue that the most vital kit of all will be the relevant OS map (ideally, with a waterproof cover) as well as a compass and the ability to use them both. Some very basic skills are covered here, but if you need more training do consider taking a course with one of the many very good outdoor centres in the UK, such as Glenmore Lodge (Scotland) or Plas y Brenin (Snowdonia), or perhaps taking a mountain leader or guide with you for your first experience.

Which map?

The mapping we have in the UK is some of the best in the world. Ordnance Survey are the best known, though Harvey maps (for key parts of Scotland, Wales and England) offer an alternative. They will either be 1:25,000 or 1:50,000 in scale. The latter is good for planning a long route – especially over some areas in Scotland that can span three or four maps, but the former is much better for walking the route on the ground. It shows much more detail – such as fence lines, streams and landmarks – that really help you place your location.

Getting orientated

The first thing to do when you reach your start point is orientate your map: that is, quite simply, turning it so that it matches up with what you are looking at and faces the direction in which you are going. Before you start walking, look at where you are heading and check the map to see what you should see on the way there – perhaps a waterfall, another path joining yours or a fence line. Make sure to include features that won't change, such as lakes or streams. Once you get going, mentally check these things off along the way.

Some routes may well be waymarked for a while, with signposts directing you at various intervals. You can't rely on these, however, as posts are often moved or broken, so do keep an eye on your map and know where you are and where you're heading at all times.

Planning your timings

It's important to have a sense of how long a walk should take you. A good general rule is one called Naismith's. It states that the average person walks at 4km/hour on flat ground, so a 4km walk should take around an hour.

Add an extra ten minutes for every 100m uphill, and 30 minutes of breaks for every four hours you walk – plus a little bit more for camera stops. This rule is not set in stone, but it's a reasonable basis for planning in advance roughly how long a route should take you. It means that when on the ground you can check that you are roughly where you think you should be at any given time. Bear in mind that walking at night always takes longer than you think it should – as, for some reason, does walking in the woods.

Remember, the weather in the mountains and on high moorland can change very rapidly and confuse even the most experienced of navigators. So, in the spirit of 'enjoy not endure', if the weather for your planned wild weekend looks bad then, unless you are a confident navigator or the route is on easy, well-defined paths, you may be better off postponing your trip or heading somewhere less demanding.

GPS?

Today, an increasing number of people rely for navigation on a GPS receiver or mobile phone app. There's nothing wrong with this: they can be quick, handy tools. But you should always take a paper map and compass with you too, if only as backup. Remember that batteries don't last forever and that mobile phones are not built to survive all the rigours of the great outdoors. Make sure, also, that you test out your gadgets before you set out: you need to know how to use them – and understand their limitations – sooner rather than later.

TOILET TALK

If there's one question I get asked above all by first-time wild campers it's 'where do I go to the toilet?' The answer is simple: you go in the great outdoors! It may not be pretty to talk about but it's really not that big a deal: do it once and you'll never worry about doing it again.

Of course there's a right way to do it. One option is to carry out everything. In some places, such as the Cairngorms, in Scotland, you can collect a special 'Poo Pot' to take with you. You 'go' in that, carry it out then deposit it afterwards in one of the special bins, where it is properly cleaned. Carrying out is the best option if sleeping in a cave – somewhere you should never use as a toilet. For camping or bothying, you may prefer to dig your own hole. Bothies always provide a toilet shovel for this reason. Choose a spot at least 30m from any water source – you might want to use that later yourself – and well away from paths and bothies. Dig a small hole, around 15cm deep, then do what you need to do. You will probably have brought in your own tissue or toilet paper: you need to carry this out (along with any sanitary products; bring a sealable bag for this), as it takes a long time to break down and may well be unearthed by a wild animal. When finished, cover the hole and remember to clean your hands (hand sanitiser works well). Whatever your method, just be respectful of the wild place you're in, leave it as you would wish to find it and take out all rubbish with you.

SAFETY

Going into the wild is exhilarating and, as long as you're sensible, the chances of things going wrong are low. However, you have to be prepared to take responsibility for yourself. The following basic precautions are important.

- Whether setting out alone or with friends, always leave your plans with a responsible person. These should include a map showing your planned route and your expected time back. Some hotels and B&Bs will offer to do this for you, which is great, but you should also alert a responsible person who you know will raise the alarm if all else fails. And do remember to check in with this person and any hotels when you are back, so that they don't unnecessarily report you as missing.
- Dressing appropriately is key to staying safe and warm so never leave behind something important just to lighten your load. Also check the weather forecast before you head off. The best is ✆ www.mwis.com for mountain areas or the Met Office for the rest of the UK. Don't be scared of a last-minute change of plan if conditions are not ideal. Having a plan B and even C is always a good idea.
- It's good to know basic first aid, and remember to take your personalised first aid kit with you. Know the emergency signal: six long blasts on a whistle or six long flashes of a torch, followed by a one-minute gap and then repeated, indicates you need help.
- Mountain Rescue is a last resort – not just an option for when you feel tired. Remember that rescuers are volunteers who receive no funding. If all else fails and you do need them, call ☎ 999 and ask for the police (or coastguard, by the sea), who will be able to then get in touch with the relevant rescue team. If you can't get a signal on your mobile try calling ☎ 112: this special number is pre-programmed into every SIM card and mobile phone and, when used, will allow your phone to hunt for other service providers. It also prioritises your call to override a busy network.

Try calling for one minute. If no joy, turn 180 degrees and try again – just in case you are blocking a mast.

- You can also register to be able to text the emergency services. You must do this before you go: simply text the word 'Register' to ☎ 112. Then answer 'Yes' to the automated message you receive. This will enable you to text them later, if needed.
- If calling for help, remember to keep your back to the wind so that you can be heard properly. Speak slowly and clearly, giving your name, your location, what's happened and how many people are involved. It will help enormously if you can pinpoint your location with a grid reference. Learn how to do this before you go.
- Above all, keep reminding yourself: 'enjoy not endure'. If things are going wrong never be afraid to turn back: the wilderness will still be there next time. It's a hard call to make, but the best adventurers are the ones who know when to call it a day. And the best stories are often those when you have had to change plans: it's what being an adventurer is all about!

NOTE: The routes in this book do come with manageable risks and take place in very remote locations. The author and publisher have done all they can to ensure the accuracy of the route descriptions, but they cannot be held legally or financially responsible for any accident, injury, loss or inconvenience sustained as a result of the information or advice contained in this book. Any outdoor activity – whether walking, backpacking, wild camping or staying in caves and bothies – is always undertaken entirely at your own risk.

PERMISSION AND ETIQUETTE

Another of the most common questions I am asked about wild camping is: 'am I really allowed to do it'. When it comes to the routes in this book, wild camping is only officially permitted in Scotland and on Dartmoor. Elsewhere, you are supposed to ask the landowner's permission first. From experience, however, this is usually either impractical or impossible. Wild camping in the kind of wild places described in this book is normally tolerated, as long as you do it properly. It's all a case of etiquette. The following guidelines should help:

A wild sleeper's etiquette

- Arrive late; leave early.
- Sleep well above the wall line, away from people's houses.
- Leave no trace of your camp (take all rubbish with you).

- Save fires for the bothies; don't light them in the great outdoors and risk damaging fragile ecosystems.
- Bury your toilet waste and pack out all paper and sanitary products.
- Be respectful at all times. If asked to move on, do so.
- Always aim to leave a wild place – whether camp spot, cave, beach or bothy – in a better condition than when you found it.
- Always close gates behind you.
- If you take a dog with you, keep it on a lead around livestock or where signs indicate that you should.

Bothy etiquette

If using one of the bothies mentioned in this book, observe the following:

- Respect other people. It's not a case of first come, first served: a bothy is an open shelter for everyone, so make room when you can and remain courteous with other users. Group numbers are limited to a maximum of six. Be prepared to camp outside if the bothy is full when you arrive.
- Respect the bothy. Always take your own rubbish away – and any other rubbish you find that you can make space for. Trash breeds more trash, so don't be part of the problem: be part of the solution.
- Make sure the fire is out when you go and that the door is securely closed to stop wildlife getting inside.
- Respect the surroundings. Unless there is a composting toilet or similar on site (rare), then use the spade provided to dig a hole. Bring your own fuel; never cut live trees from around the bothy.
- Don't overstay your welcome. There's a general understanding that stays should not last for more than a couple of days. If you intend to stay longer, seek permission from the landowner first.
- Pay attention to restrictions: some bothies are closed during stag/grouse hunting seasons, and this will be clearly noted either on the building or the Mountain Bothies Association website (🖱 www.mountainbothies.org.uk).

Cave sleeping

Caves are damp so it's a good idea to take a bivvy bag for your sleeping bag, as well as some tarp or a groundsheet to protect your camping mat and provide extra insulation. These natural bedrooms can change over time so it's best to recce them before you bed down for the night, just in case they are no longer suitable. Always take your tent and be prepared to camp in case the cave is already occupied or no longer appears safe.

USING THIS GUIDE

In this book you will find a collection of 26 of the best wild weekends that I think Britain has to offer. Each one features maps to help you plan a good walk-in and an excellent adventure, plus photographs to illustrate the kind of landscape and attractions you are likely to experience. The directions of the suggested route are described in detail, but you do need to check these out on a proper OS map before setting off (and take the map with you). And don't be afraid to adapt the directions to your needs and ability, especially if you find the path has changed. A longer and shorter option is included for most sites, as are my suggestions on the best time for you to go.

In an attempt to be as carbon-free as possible, I have included details of any possible public transport for reaching the route. With some routes this is more practical than with others. Again, do check these options before you leave, as timetables and services are subject to change. Some wild places are so far off the beaten track – which is, after all their attraction – that public transport is simply not feasible.

WILD LAND, WILDLIFE

One of the joys of heading into the more remote and rugged corners of the UK is coming across some of our native wildlife. The route descriptions here mention a few of the more conspicuous or interesting species you might encounter. But this is by no means an exhaustive list, and you are bound to see more. Keep your eyes peeled. Wildlife or plant enthusiasts might want to pack a small field guide or – especially for birdwatchers – a lightweight pair of binoculars.

PLAN YOUR OWN WILDERNESS WEEKEND

With luck, after trying some of the weekends described here, you'll be ready to plan and enjoy your own adventure. So how do you go about it? First, get an OS map – whether of your local area or your favourite national park. Scrutinise it for spots away from houses and built-up areas. Look for flattened-top hillsides and handy water sources, such as streams and tarns. Then recce the place by daylight, to make sure it lives up to your expectations. Have a plan 'B' – and 'C': if the place you've found isn't suitable, or there's someone already there, it's worth having alternatives up your sleeve. Keep your Go Bag (see page 17) packed, of course, and watch the weather. Then, once you get the window you want, you have no excuses not to go for it!

Once there, don't stress. The first time you wild camp or sleep in a cave/ bothy, it's completely normal to imagine the worst: that the rustling you hear outside is a murderer or (unaccountably, in the UK) a bear. Trust me: it's a rabbit. Or, at worst, a sheep.

Why not share your adventure? If you've had a great experience following one of the routes in this book, you can use it as a springboard to plan your own wild weekend then tell other people all about it. Tweet on 🐦 **#wildernessweekends** and we'll retweet it for you!

A WORD ABOUT THE SITE SELECTION

The 26 routes featured in this book have been selected on the basis that you can complete each within a single weekend. This allows you to integrate a regular dose of the wild into your working life without having to eat into your holidays. Most weekends, however, have the potential for longer exploration, should you find yourself with more time on your hands, so suggestions for extending your visit are included.

You may wonder, after a glance at the map on page 4, why the book shows such an apparent northerly and westerly bias, with its 26 routes clustered primarily in Dartmoor, Wales, the Lake District and Scotland. This does not, of course, mean that there are no wild places in southern and eastern England. But it does reflect a certain two-part reality. First: the UK's wildest areas are in upland regions – those landscapes that have proved rugged enough over the centuries to resist the heaviest farming and development – and one glance at our topography reveals that such lofty regions are located almost entirely in the west and far north. Second: it is in these areas, generally furthest from our largest centres of population, that wild camping is least intrusive and thus most practical and most acceptable. In other upland regions – for example, the Peak District and North York Moors – the hiking may be excellent but wild camping is generally prohibited or at least frowned upon. You are, of course, more than welcome to investigate other possibilities, heeding the general guidance on etiquette and safety.

As a London resident myself, I make no apologies for having to travel a little distance for my wild weekends. The good news is that, wherever you live in our crowded little country, genuine wilderness may be closer than you think. London lies no more than four hours from South Wales or Dartmoor, while from Birmingham and Manchester it is just a short hop to North Wales and the Lakes, and Glasgow stands at the gateway to the Scottish Highlands – one of the most remote corners of Europe. Wherever you go, go prepared and you will have the adventure of a lifetime.

FEEDBACK REQUEST AND UPDATES WEBSITE

At Bradt Travel Guides we're aware that guidebooks start to go out of date on the day they're published – and that you, our readers, are out there in the field doing research of your own. So why not write and tell us about your experiences? Contact us on ☎ 01753 893444 or @ info@bradtguides.com. We will forward emails to the author who may post updates on the Bradt website at 🖱 www.bradtupdates.com/wildernessweekends. Alternatively you can add a review of the book to 🖱 www.bradtguides.com or Amazon.

⛰ Waking up to wilderness is a more realistic prospect than many UK-dwellers imagine.

> **FLANKED BY RISING CLIFFS OF BURNT CRIMSON ON ONE SIDE AND THE RHYTHMIC LAPPING OF WAVES ON THE OTHER, THERE COULD BE FEW BETTER PLACES TO SPEND THE NIGHT**

ENGLAND

1 DO-IT-YOURSELF DRIFTWOOD DEN

BUILD YOUR OWN SHELTER BENEATH
THE CLIFFS ON PEPPERCOMBE BEACH, DEVON

WHERE	Peppercombe, Devon
DURATION	1 night, 2 days
START/FINISH	Lay-by just east of Horns Cross **♀** SS384231
MAPS	OS Landranger (1:50,000) 190; OS Explorer (1:25,000) 126

As children, most of us built dens. We spent hours crafting our mini-houses from sticks and leaves, perfecting these temporary shelters until, finally, it was time to return home and have our tea. This adventure starts in just the same way – but this time round, happily, building a den is only the beginning. This time you'll actually get to spend the night in your creation.

Along the stretch of coastline between the delightfully named town of Westward Ho! (exclamation mark included) and the ancient portside hamlet of Clovelly is one of the most beautifully secluded beaches in the UK: Peppercombe. Flanked by rising cliffs of burnt crimson on one side and the rhythmic lapping of the waves on the other, with a wave-polished expanse of shingle at your feet, there could be few better places to spend the night.

And I'm not the only one to think so. There is a long history of people coming here to build their makeshift beach bothies along the shoreline, making use of whatever materials the waves deposit among the giant pebbles. Depending upon when you visit, you can find anything from a rudimentary stick shack leant against the rocky cliffs to constructions of shed-like solidity, complete with working doors and even windows. Of course, there are also people who come here to dismantle these structures, and – given their exposed location – many also fall victim to the elements. Wild shelters are, after all, only ever a temporary affair.

When I arrived to build my own bothy I found the wreckage of many other formerly grand structures, now merely driftwood and fishing spoil broken on the sand. Then I came across a half-finished shack, so perfect the builders had even gathered fresh leaves for a pillow. I set to work filling in the gaps with a selection of bamboo stems that I'd found a kilometre away and some large rocks to secure it against the westerly breeze. Then I met the creators: two small boys who told me that every year they come with their family to this same spot and mastermind a structure in which they would like to sleep. They had never been allowed to spend the night in their creation but – they told me with

> **" I FOUND THE WRECKAGE OF MANY OTHER FORMERLY GRAND STRUCTURES, NOW MERELY DRIFTWOOD AND FISHING SPOIL "**

glee – I would be welcome to stay, have my dinner in it and sleep over if I liked. Then they left me to it.

The hours passed and I lit a fire in the small pit the boys had carefully made. The beach bothy was only a short distance from the mini-waterfall where the stream at Horns Cross makes its way down the valley to join the sea, so I had a natural shower on tap. There was not another soul for miles, and I spent the most peaceful night being lulled to sleep by the waves.

After leaving the beach, you can enjoy an excellent walk along the easy-to-follow South West Coast Path (SWCP). Heading up through the oak woodland between Peppercombe and Buck's Mills, you feel like you're somewhere with a real story to tell. Some impressive old trees cling to the steep cliff edges, having managed to escape the axe that felled their companions elsewhere. Rare species of lichen festoon their ancient limbs, while marsh orchids are among the wild flowers that grow on the forest floor beneath. Look out for peregrine falcons and ravens riding the cliff updraughts, and in spring listen for the tinkling songs of redstarts. This whole area is protected as a Site of Specific Scientific Interest.

Even the less wild parts of this walk feel suitably remote. Buck's Mills, through which you will pass *en route* to Clovelly, features old lime kilns – now crumbling into the sea – along with a handful of houses and the tiny former stone artist's cabin of Judith Ackland and Mary Stella Edwards. (The two women lived and worked there until 1971; the building is now in the care of the National Trust.) After passing through more woodland, you'll finally arrive at the quirky village of Clovelly, lining a steep scar of a valley. The picturesque cobbled streets do not allow access by vehicle, so supplies come on a sledge or the back of a donkey. It's the perfect place to arrive via the most traditional method: your boots.

The wild woodland above Peppercombe ⋏
Harbour at Clovelly (Rolf E. Staerk/S) ➤

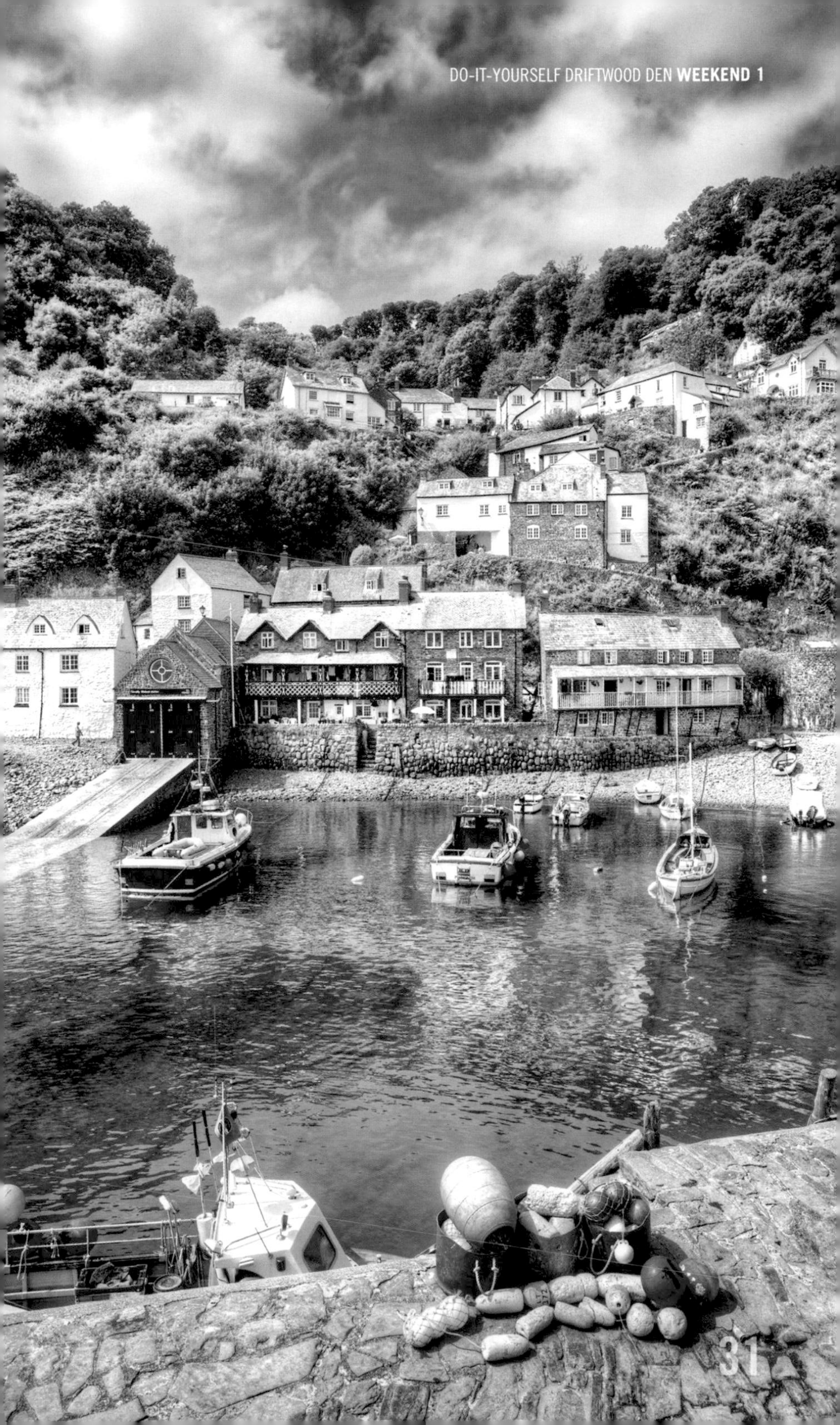

HERE'S THE PLAN
DAY 1

1 From the lay-by, head west along the road towards the village centre. At the pub turn right down the road. It soon forks. The path on the right becomes a gravel track blocked by a gate. Go through this and follow the track downhill until you come to the SWCP. Ignore this for now and continue straight on, following signs for the beach. You'll pass a building on your left and go through a gate, then some trees, before finally emerging onto the beach.

2 Peppercombe is the perfect place for a beach sleep. Make sure you stay above the waterline, on the flattened rocks near the cliffs – checking above that nothing is loose or hanging precariously. It's worth bringing a groundsheet or some tarp, as the rocks can be rough, but the sunsets more than make up for it.

DAY 2

3 From the beach, retrace your steps back up through the trees, gate and onto the crossroads where the SWCP intersects the track up to Horns Cross. This time turn right to head west onto the National Trail. This starts off uphill and then weaves around the ancient woodland, offering tantalising glimpses of the sea. After a couple of kilometres the path begins to descend into the village of Buck's Mills.

4 Take a minute to wander down to the sea front and check out the old lime kiln, a remnant of the industry that put this place on the map. Then head back uphill and rejoin the SWCP. Continue as it weaves in and

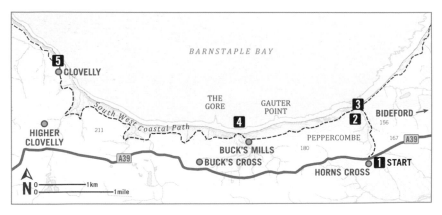

around the woodland for several more kilometres until you arrive in the quaint village of Clovelly, with its cobbled streets and donkeys.

5 Take some time to explore. Then either retrace your steps or, better yet, walk up to the visitor centre to catch the bus back to your start.

TOP TIP Beach bothies can be cold and damp – or non-existent – so make sure you take a bivvy bag in case you need a plan B. For water, look for where the river descends to the beach (to the right of the entrance) or carry in enough for the night.

⋀ Water on tap on Peppercombe beach

NUTS AND BOLTS

PRE-TRIP Other than a pub meal, you'll find no food to buy in Horns Cross. Your best bet for supplies is Bideford, which has many supermarkets and shops, plus a range of accommodation options.

PUBLIC TRANSPORT A handy bus route runs between Hartland and Barnstaple: Stagecoach line 319 (approx four times a day; less frequent on Sunday). This stops at both Clovelly and Horns Cross, making a linear walk fairly straightforward. National Rail connects Barnstable to the rest of the UK.

WHEN TO GO This coast can be a great place to spend a night year-round but, whatever the season, check that the conditions are calm enough to be able to enjoy a restful night. Watch the tide chart closely, stick to low tides and keep an eye on the weather.

IF YOU DON'T FANCY THE BEACH BOTHY? If you'd rather not stay on the beach then you will find some flat spots among the woods above Peppercombe, just off the SWCP. Be careful if pitching among trees: choose the side of the path away from the cliffs and try to pick an area away from the canopy, where there is less chance of an old, rotten branch tumbling on you.

SHORT OF TIME? You could either just walk in, camp and walk out again, or – for a shorter walk – just go as far as Buck's Mills then walk up to the main road and catch the bus back.

TIME TO SPARE? With 1,000km (630 miles) of the SWCP running in both directions from your campsite, the choice is yours. Check out the cliffs and beachside towns to the north around Westward Ho! or continue past Clovelly to Hartland Head and the wild headland beyond.

MORE INFO
Clovelly ☺ www.clovelly.co.uk
SWCP ☺ www.southwestcoastpath.com
Local ☺ www.hartlandpeninsula.co.uk

Marsh marigolds in spring (ArjaKo's/S) ⋏
View from the South West Coast Path (Patricia Hofmeester/S) ➢

WHERE	Erme Plains, Dartmoor
DURATION	1 night, 2 days
START/FINISH	Harford village car park ♀ SX643595
MAPS	OS Landranger (1:50,000) 202; OS Explorer (1:25,000) 20, 28

I f you've already pored over the OS map that covers this area then you don't need me to tell you that its history reaches back a long way. From stone rows to old settlements, cairns, hut circles and remains from several centuries of tin mining, humankind's relationship with this picturesque part of Dartmoor National Park is written all over the landscape. Boasting the largest concentration of Bronze-Age spoils in the UK, historians believe that the moorlands up here were once among the country's most populous. Back then much of the area was covered in trees, but – as all over Britain – most have since been felt to make way for farming or cleared for livestock.

2 AMONG ANCIENT STONES

DISCOVER A LOST VILLAGE ON DARTMOOR, DEVON

On Dartmoor, the result of all this forest clearance was to make the ground even more peaty and boggy, and now you can't walk more than a few metres without feeling the moors tremble beneath your feet. There is, however, one other noticeable feature of the landscape, and that's the granite tors. These wind-scoured summits were once merely exposed hilltops, devoid of the vegetation that surrounded them. They

> **"**
> **NOW YOU CAN'T WALK MORE THAN A FEW METRES WITHOUT FEELING THE MOORS TREMBLE BENEATH YOUR FEET**
> **"**

have since been sculpted by the elements into otherworldly shapes that are unique to this part of the world, and have survived the tests of time rather better than the manmade ruins that are scattered around them.

Today, people keen to learn more about our ancestors head to Dartmoor for a glimpse into our past. Among the prehistoric structures that remain, one the most impressive is found on Erme Plains: the Upper Erme Stone Row. Stretching in a perfect line for over 3,320m, this is the longest stone

Forget Stonehenge: this is Erme Plains

row not only in the national park but also the whole world. Towards its southern end is a stone circle made up of 26 rocks. Known locally as The Dancers, legend has it that these were once local girls who came up to the moor on a Sunday to dance, and were turned to stone as punishment for this grievous sin and as a warning to others tempted to do the same.

Now it's not dancers that come here, but walkers. And there are no permanent homesteads and huts, only temporary shelters in the form of tents. Dartmoor, you see, is the one place in England where, thanks to a local byelaw, you can legally pitch up for a wild camp – as long as you do so properly and respectfully (ie: 100m from a road, not on an archaeological site, and not in an area enclosed by walls). This opens a real door for adventure. You can now wander among the ruins, on the very plains where our ancestors used to smelt tin, shelter in stone huts and secure their animals, and imagine just how it felt to be part of one of those ancient communities.

Be sure to watch for wildlife while you're up here. You might spy buzzards overhead, Dartmoor ponies trotting by, curious rabbits or badgers at your tent flaps, or adders and grass snakes on the wetlands by the river. The ancients may be long gone but there's still plenty of life on the moor yet.

HERE'S THE PLAN
DAY 1

1 From the car park head onto the open moorland in an easterly direction. You should soon find a path. Wide in places and narrow in others, it passes over mainly boggy ground and long grass. Follow this, ignoring any turn-offs or cattle tracks, until you get to the unmistakably wide track of the Two Moors Way footpath, which cuts north to south.

2 Follow the Two Moors Way footpath north, along Ugborough Moor. If it's late, the land to the right of the main footpath, before the stone rows, can be a good place to pitch your tent. Otherwise continue, not being afraid to leave the track to check out the tors and cairns either side. You'll cut under the lower flanks of Three Barrows – a high point of 464m – but keep on until the path swings round to the right and you reach an old bridge.

Dartmoor ponies (eelnosiva/S) ▲

3 This is a great spot to stop for a bite to eat and soak up what life must have been like working in the old quarry. Explore a little and you will see the old tracks that transported the spoils in and out. When you're ready, continue on the track until it takes a sharp turn northeast. As the track bends you'll see a faint path that continues north-northwest. Follow this, making a beeline for Erme Plains.

4 It's here that you are presented with a wonderful collection of old settlements, stone circles and cairns. Follow the faint riverside path until the river narrows near some rocks. Then cross on the makeshift stepping stones. From here make a beeline uphill. It's hard-going but soon you will reach what looks like a few pieces of a stone row.

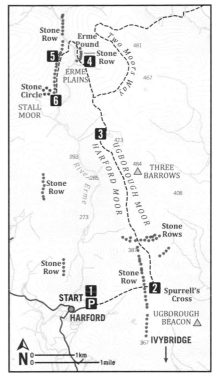

5 Look north and south and you will realise that this is no ordinary stone row; in fact it's the longest one in Britain. Follow it south until you reach a stone circle. This is a magical place to pitch a tent nearby, with none of the crowds or coaches you get at Stonehenge.

DAY 2

6 Making sure you leave no trace of your visit, retrace your steps to the point where you crossed the river yesterday and cross there. (It gets harder to ford the further south you go.) Then simply follow your outward journey in reverse back to the start.

TOP TIP If you want to walk out by a different route from the one by which you arrived, you can continue south up on Stall Moor and pick up the path that runs alongside the west bank of the River Erme. It will take you back to the road that leads to Harford. The downside is a 2.5km road walk back to Harford. The choice is yours.

NUTS AND BOLTS

PRE-TRIP Ivybridge is the best and nearest town in which to pick up supplies. There are a couple of supermarkets and smaller shops, not to mention a chippy if you fancy something hot and calorific before your adventure.

PUBLIC TRANSPORT At present there are no public transport options to get you to the start. However, you could take a train to Ivybridge (☉ www.nationalrail.co.uk) then either get a taxi for the 5km to the start or pick up the Two Moors Way National Trail that starts in the town to join this route at step 2.

WHEN TO GO No matter what time of year you go, try to pick a day/night when it's dry. The ground is often very saturated, so winter can be a good option if there's a frost – although it does get cold on the open moorland. Summer can be wonderful, especially after a dry period.

IF YOU DON'T FANCY THE STONE CIRCLE? In Dartmoor wild camping is perfectly legal as long as you do so responsibly, and far from anyone's houses. The land around Ugborough Beacon offers great views down to Ivybridge so is a great place to pitch; the old bridge at step 3 is another option, and conveniently next to a water source.

SHORT OF TIME?
You needn't go all the way to Erme to find stone circles and settlements. Just a short walk from Harford car park there are tors and hut circles, and not long after you meet the Two Moors Way you will find remains of stone rows and classic wind-scoured tors. Perfect to explore if time is tight.

TIME TO SPARE?
Dartmoor has endless possibilities. Beyond Erme Plains are more hut remains and old bridges, not to mention crosses and circles. Just remember to take your map and compass – and know how to use them, as Dartmoor can be difficult to navigate if the fog comes in.

MORE INFO
Ivybridge ✪ www.ivybridge-devon.co.uk
National Park ✪ www.dartmoor-npa.gov.uk
Dartmoor ✪ www.dartmoor.co.uk
Wild camping on Dartmoor Guidance ✪ www.dartmoor.gov.uk/visiting/
vi-enjoyingdartmoor/camping

Bowerman's Nose is is one of many granite stacks found in Dartmoor's wild landscapes. (ASC Photography/S)

3 BEWARE OF THE BEASTS

WANDER IN THE PHANTOM PAW-PRINTS OF THE FAMOUS HOUND ON DARTMOOR, DEVON

WHERE	Hound Tor and Grimspound, Dartmoor
DURATION	1 night, 2 days
START/FINISH	Hound Tor car park ♥ SX739792
MAPS	OS Landranger (1:50,000) 191; OS Explorer (1:25,000) 28

These days Dartmoor has another claim to fame, beside its granite tors and Neolithic structures: big cats. Since 1976, when the Dangerous Wild Animals Act made it illegal to keep wild animals as pets, the moors have seen a flurry of sightings, supposedly of escaped or released large felines. From panther and puma to leopard and lynx: you name it, someone has, apparently, some blurred footage of it. In 2011 alone there were 14 different reports of a large black cat nicknamed the 'Beast of Dartmoor' in this national park.

Not that tales of dangerous predators are anything new. Fans of literature will know that Sir Arthur Conan Doyle created the character of Sherlock Holmes and penned the celebrated story of *The Hound of the Baskervilles*, set in this very part of England. Since then, Dartmoor has been synonymous with spectral canines roaming the moors.

Nobody has ever proved conclusively that these rogue canines or felines are anything more than the products of their author's – or the local newspapers' – imagination. But if you want to try spotting one for yourself, you need only head to one of Dartmoor's most famous tors. Situated off the B3387, between the villages of Bovey Tracey and Widecombe-in-the-Moor, sits the massive outcrop of Hound Tor. The name of this weathered granite lump comes from its resemblance to the heads of a group of dogs, the unfortunate animals having been turned into stone by an angry witch when they spilled her cauldron while chasing a hare – or so local legend has it.

> **IT IS SAID THAT IN 1638 THE DEVIL HIMSELF VISITED THIS UNASSUMING VILLAGE**

While you may need even more of an active imagination to see this likeness than you would to spot a spectral hound, the tor certainly can't be beaten as a starting point for exploring this northern end of Dartmoor. On the map, there appears to be a network of roads spanning the moors, but after five minutes off the tourist trail you will find a very wild place all to yourself. Following a camp beneath the rocks above the remains of the deserted medieval village of Hundatora (abandoned in the mid 1300s), you continue to the aforementioned Widecombe. Here, if local legend is

◄ The dog-like rocks at Hound Tor (David Brian Williamson/S)

anything to go by, wild animals are the least of your problems: it is said that in 1638 the Devil himself visited this unassuming village, bringing tragedy to its occupants. In reality it was a violent thunderstorm, striking the church when a service was in full swing, that was responsible for killing four people and injuring a whole lot more.

Continue past Widecombe to walk amongst the giant Bronze-Age settlement of Grimspound. Thought to have been established in 1300BC, its remains now consist of 24 stone hut circles within a mammoth perimeter wall. Archaeologists believe this enclosure housed cattle rather than people, and its walls served to keep out the wind – and predators, real or imagined.

Persisting with the supernatural theme, before reaching the end of this venture you'll pass the supposedly haunted Jay's Grave. This raised burial mound is said to be that of a woman who committed suicide and was therefore not afforded a spot in a Christian graveyard. Stories abound in local history, both by word of mouth and literature. The main mystery once concerned the source of the flowers that would regularly appear on her grave. Once said to be the work of pixies, the person responsible was in reality Beatrice Chase, a local author. Chase has since passed away, but visitors from all over keep up her tradition and make offerings to this unmarked resting place.

Many of the local legends around this area may be based on phantoms and apparitions, but one thing's for sure: the setting for this ethereal wild sleep is most definitely real.

HERE'S THE PLAN
DAY 1

1 Starting at the car park, head towards the giant tors on the horizon in front of you. This whole area is a beautiful place to pitch, but if you can resist then continue instead past the boulderers and rock climbers on the granite and head towards Greator. Few will come this way and even the ones that do will stop in front of it, perhaps climb it, then head back to the car park. This area offers much better spots to pitch, either behind the tor or on one of the many flat and secluded areas that encircle it.

DAY 2

2 Continue south, heading downhill past your nightspot and following the path as it swings from south to west and emerges onto the minor road near Holwell Lawn. Cross this road and pick up the path on the other side to take you further southwest.

3 As you reach the next road make a right and take the lower path, onto the bridleway heading northwest, then north along the lower flanks of Bell Tor.

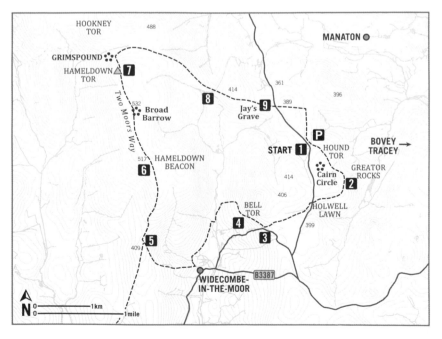

4 Where the path forks, follow the lower fork further downhill and onto the road. Turn left along the road and follow it for a little over a kilometre until you reach the small hamlet of Widecombe-in-the-Moor. Before the church, take the steep road that heads west uphill and, where it ends after about 500m, pick up the footpath and continue up onto the moorland.

5 You'll arrive at a crossroads of paths. Take the one on your right, heading north. This is the Two Moors Way, which descends a little before re-ascending steadily uphill to Hameldown Beacon. Here you'll get some cracking views across to Hound Tor, where you began your journey yesterday.

6 Keep on the main track, ignoring all smaller/fainter turn-offs, following the ridgeline as it bears north-northwest. You'll pass the marker stone at Broad Barrow, then the remains of the cross at Hameldown Cross, before reaching the cairn on Hameldown Tor. From here, you'll get your first glimpse of Grimspound, the remains of a huge Bronze-Age settlement.

7 Walk downhill and explore all you want, before turning right onto the track that heads northeast then southeast, bringing you – about 1.5km later – onto the minor road.

8 Cross this road and pick up the path directly ahead. Soon you'll emerge onto another minor road and see the unmistakable mound of Jay's Grave in front of you.

9 Cross the road and continue east over the moor, keeping a lookout for the Dartmoor ponies which roam freely in this area. When you arrive at the next minor road, turn right onto it and follow it south for about 600m. At the crossroads turn left to arrive back to the car park at Hound Tor and your start point.

TOP TIP If you arrive on day 1 with a full day ahead but need to get off earlier on day 2, you can always start the walk at Grimspound, where there's a small car-parking area (a lay-by). Then do the walk in reverse, camping near to Hound Tor. This means you can wake up, perhaps pick up some breakfast from the trailer in the car park – named, hilariously, 'Hound of the Basket Meals' – and then take the much shorter route back to your car, past Jay's Grave and over the moor to Grimspound.

A sunny spring day on Dartmoor brings out adders (MF Photo/S)

A howling good camp spot near Hound Tor

NUTS AND BOLTS

PRE-TRIP You will need to collect supplies pre-trip; the temporary kiosk has some food but its opening hours are unpredictable, especially out of summer. Try the nearby town of Bovey Tracey for snacks and food. For camping supplies, you'll be better off in Newton Abbot or – if arriving from the north – Exeter.

PUBLIC TRANSPORT Very infrequent. It's relatively easy to get buses to either nearby Bovey Tracey or Moretonhampstead but then the only option is line 671 with Carmel Coaches (🐭 www.carmelcoaches.co.uk), which will get you to Becky Falls, 2km away. This runs only once a week, on Wednesdays.

WHEN TO GO This is a great walk at any time of the year. August, when purple heather brings the moorland alive with colour, is particularly recommended.

IF YOU DON'T FANCY THE CAMPING SPOT? There are lots of other places that are perfect for a pitch. Try the high land on Hamel Down or the flat area near the summits of Hookney Tor for views over to Grimspound. Collect and purify water where you can, as most good wild camp spots are not close to water sources.

SHORT OF TIME? A visit to Hound Tor or Grimspound and back are the two highlights that easily work as a shorter day trip, or you could just take your tent and enjoy a quick overnight wild camp near to Hound Tor.

TIME TO SPARE? With its liberal stance on wild camping, Dartmoor is *the* place to explore. Make sure you have a map and compass though, and remember that in mist – which can descend year-round – navigation can be tricky.

MORE INFO
Wild camping www.dartmoor.co.uk/where-to-stay/dartmoor-camping/wild-camping-on-dartmoor
Dartmoor www.dartmoor-npa.gov.uk
Local www.visitsouthdevon.co.uk
Hound Tor/Grimspound www.english-heritage.org.uk

Heather brings a splash of colour to the rugged moorland

WHERE	Pendle, Lancashire
DURATION	1 night, 2 days
START/FINISH	Barley car park ⚲ SD823403
MAPS	OS Landranger (1:50,000) 103; OS Explorer (1:25,000) 41, 21

You'd expect an ancient hill to come with a momentous history. But none seems to come with quite as much as a single, isolated peak that sits in the heart of Lancashire. Beyond the gritstone edges of the Peak District, below the rolling heather of the Yorkshire Dales, separated from the Pennines and the Forest of Bowland's fells, stands one Pendle Hill.

Not only was this clay and peat gritstone mass the peak on which a man called George Fox had a vision that led him in 1652 to form the Quakers but, 40 years earlier, it also set the scene for England's biggest witch hunt.

4 WITCH HUNT WANDERINGS

BIVVY ON A HILL WHERE THE WITCH TRIALS TOOK PLACE, PENDLE, LANCASHIRE

Pre-dating the hysteria that swept through Salem and New England by some 80 years, the Pendle Witch Trials of 1612 resulted in ten locals being hanged, high on the moors in front of a baying crowd.

The trouble started in March 1612 when a local girl called Alizon Device was out begging on the hill. When the man she accosted refused to help her she muttered a curse. The man collapsed and was rendered temporarily paralysed. Nowadays, of course, it's assumed he merely had a stroke, but back then, when being labelled a local 'wise woman' could mean a boost in income through selling cures, curses and spells, poor Alizon admitted to witchcraft. As if that wasn't bad enough, during her confession she implicated a host of other members of the Pendle community – including one called Old Demdike, a known 'wise woman', and members of her own family.

> **"40 YEARS EARLIER, IT ALSO SET THE SCENE FOR ENGLAND'S BIGGEST WITCH HUNT"**

Pendle Hill bathed in a glow of Halloween orange (albinoni/S)

Most of the accused were poor, and were probably caught up in a wave of hysteria, finger-pointing and bribery. One, however, was different. Alice Nutter – whose statue now stands on the side of the road in her former home village of Roughlee – was a wealthy widow who, local historians believe, was the victim of a row over land ownership with the magistrate leading the trial. Poor Alice, it is said, was well and truly stitched up. By 20 August that same year all but one (who was sentenced to the stocks) of the 12 accused were dead. It is hard to know what really happened: the one surviving document from the time is heavily biased in favour of the courts, while local folklore and contradictory theories cloud the truth. The discovery in 2011 of the remains of a mummified cat entombed in the wall of an old cottage didn't help matters.

Although the events that surround the trials took place in a number of locations across the Pendle area, it's the hill itself that still bewitches visitors. Its appeal has generated everything from local ghost tours to the infamous visit of the *Most Haunted* TV crew in 2004, and every year there's even a fancy-dress pilgrimage up to the highest point.

Despite the kitsch in the villages below, however, especially come Halloween, this does feel like a truly wild place once you head uphill. Sequestered from any other high ground by the natural barriers of rivers and valleys, the summit is a world all its own. On a clear day it offers outstanding views as far as the towns of Blackburn, Preston and even Blackpool. The grass and moorland seem to stretch for miles, while paragliders swoop overhead – often in the company of birds of prey, including buzzards, kestrels, sparrowhawks and the occasional short-eared owl. In spring, keen birdwatchers may even spy dotterels using the hill as a pit stop on their long journey north.

But the best time to be there by far is at night. Then, when the sky turns to flame with the setting sun, you can sit on your high island-like viewpoint and watch as, one by one, the lights of the surrounding towns and villages switch on, like a sprinkling of ground-level stars. As you snuggle up in your bivvy to enjoy the light play from your little hump of wildness, it won't be witchcraft that enchants you and sends you off to sleep, but the landscape itself.

Alice Nutter greets visitors to Roughlee ◀

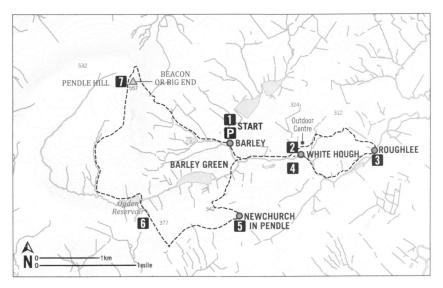

HERE'S THE PLAN
DAY 1

1 From the car park at Barley turn left, heading away from the village. Almost immediately you will see a sign directing you onto the Pendle Way footpath on your left (marked with marker posts featuring  witches). Follow this track, passing through the cobbled streets and stone houses of Narrowgates Mill, until you come to White Hough.

2 At White Hough, turn left to head north, walking up past the houses. At the top of the street turn right and follow the road as it curves round uphill to the left. Just before you reach the Outdoor Centre, after a small redbrick building, you will see the footpath markers on your right. Follow these into the woods. It's an eerie meander through the trees for about 500m until you reach open farmland. Continue to the minor road, turn left uphill for a short while and then right along the track. Keep following signs for the Pendle Way around Croft House Farm, at which point you follow the path southwest, heading downhill across fields all the way to Blacko Bar Road.

3 At Blacko Bar Road, turn right and take the pavement to follow the road into Roughlee, home of Alice Nutter. You'll pass the Old Hall (where some claim she lived), the statue of her in shackles and a fingerpost pointing towards Lancaster Castle, the place where all the witches were sentenced to death. Carefully, continuing along the road, turn right onto the footpath immediately after you've crossed the bridge. Follow this, keeping to the left bank of the river.

4 You'll soon find yourself back at White Hough. Rejoin the Pendle Way to lead you back into Barley. Pass the car park and cross the road to follow the road signed for Barley Green. You'll come to a footbridge on your left. Take this to cross the stream then follow the footpath that leads uphill, passing diagonally below the farmhouse. Continue uphill to reach a Pendle Way sign. Turn left to join the footpath and follow this downhill into Newchurch in Pendle.

5 If you need to pick up a map or a snack (or a witch's cauldron), you can turn left up the main village road to Witches Galore – worth a look to meet its wonderful owners alone. Otherwise turn right to pass St Mary's Church, where you'll find the Witches Grave and the 'Eye of God', a carving on a church steeple. Continue onto Well Head Road to pass Faugh's Quarry, the place where Demdike was said to have sold her soul to the Devil. Passing the Christian Centre on your left and a farm on your right, take the stile onto the footpath that follows the wall line uphill. As it flattens out

TOP Short-eared owls fly by day (Peter Moore) ⋀
BOTTOM Pendle Hill summit at sunset

> **TOP TIP** Although the map shows water sources to be around 500m from the summit, these will be difficult to find and reach when night falls. To be on the safe side, take plenty of water with you for your summit sleep.

you will find yourself overlooking Ogden Clough (below you) and the mysterious Pendle Hill (rising in front of you).

6 Now you've spent the day wandering the places that make up the backstory, it's time to tackle the legendary hill itself. Continue downhill to the reservoir. Once past its eastern end turn left to join the Pendle Way. This takes you first west alongside the water, then uphill, along Boar Clough, before swinging northwest, then north, to the summit of Pendle Hill called Beacon or Big End. This is your bivvy spot for the evening.

DAY 2

7 From the summit continue north on the Pendle Way. This soon veers northeast, before joining a path that runs southeast–northwest. Turn right onto this to head southeast, back downhill towards Barley. You'll pass Pendle House, where you come to a bigger track. Turn right onto this, then shortly afterwards left, following the Pendle Way further downhill, past Brown House and Mirewater Trout Fishery, eventually to rejoin the main road at Barley. Turn right onto this to take you back to the car park and your start point.

▲ View from Pendle Hill (Phil MacD Photography/S)

NUTS AND BOLTS

PRE-TRIP Barley offers subsistence in the form of The Pendle Inn pub, a great place to fill up on a hot dish of Demdike's Grills or Nutter's Nibbles and sup Witches' Brew ale before you head up to the summit. For snacks during the day there's The Cabin, which also sells maps and books about the area. For camping supplies the nearest outdoor store is in Accrington. Otherwise Blackburn is your best bet.

PUBLIC TRANSPORT From Manchester, Lancashire Bus's X43 (aka The Witch Way) runs to Nelson. From here, local services connect to Barrowford and on to Roughlee, Barley and Newchurch in Pendle (🖰 www.traveline-northwest.co.uk).

WHEN TO GO You can enjoy summit-sleeping, walking and witch-hunting year-round in Pendle: the landscape looks spectacular under fresh snow as well as in sunshine. An annual fancy dress pilgrimage up Pendle Hill every Halloween (31 October) raises money for the local hospice, so you may get a slightly less peaceful night's sleep if you go on that particular night!

IF YOU DON'T FANCY THE SUMMIT? Look at the map: there are certainly lower options for a wild camp, though you will need to be discreet and respectful of other people's property. If you'd rather stay in more comfort there's a campsite that also offers log cabins at Barley (🖱 www.boothmanpark.co.uk).

SHORT OF TIME? If just a quick-fire summit sleep is what you're after and you don't have time for the witch hunt before, simply park your car (considerately) at the lay-by on Barley Lane, near the track for Pendleside. From there you can take the footpath to Pendle House then follow the Pendle Way up to the summit. Short and sweet.

TIME TO SPARE? There's certainly more walking to be had in the Pendle area. However, for something that feels a lot wilder, head north to the Forest of Bowland. Once out of bounds to hikers — the gamekeepers were notorious for protecting their private land — the Countryside Rights of Way Act (2000) changed all that. Now you have the right to wander and explore the gritstone and peat that make up these fells. Even better, you'll hardly meet another soul.

MORE INFO

Local 🖱 www.visitpendle.com
Area info and Pendle Witch trial 🖱 www.visitlancashire.com

5 LOST IN THE LAKES

OVERNIGHT IN A SHEPHERD'S HUT
IN A HIDDEN CORNER OF THE LAKE DISTRICT

WHERE	Mosedale, Lake District
DURATION	1 night, 2 days
START/FINISH	Swindale Foot car park ♥ NY521141
MAPS	OS Landranger (1:50,000) 90; OS Explorer (1:25,000) 5, 7

O f all the valleys in all of Lakeland, Mosedale is the one that feels least like the national park. Accessed best from the small, remote hamlet of Swindale, as soon as you step from your car you can't help but say – like Dorothy in *The Wizard of Oz* – 'I'm not in the Lake District anymore'. You are, of course, but this area is so neglected by all but the most hardy of fell-lovers that you could spend an entire weekend walking these peaks and the valley below without so much as passing another human being.

It all starts right from the beginning. To preserve the wild feel of the area, parking is not allowed at the trail head, meaning that those who want a taste of this place have to be prepared to put in the effort. There are no tea rooms or gear shops, and no tarmacked car park with an extortionately high fee; just a simple patch of land and a sign advising that beyond this point you will find nowhere to leave a vehicle. The first few kilometres can make you question whether or not it's worth it, as you plod over the minor road, passing farm building after farm building. But then you turn a corner and the start of this untouched corner of one of our best-known national parks greets you.

> **FEW WILL GET TO SEE THE STARS COME OUT IN THIS LOST LAKELAND VALLEY**

Mosedale is a hanging valley. It owes its very existence to a glacier, which, during the last ice age, left evidence of its progress in the form of drumlins – hills formed of glacially transported debris – and carved crags at the valley head. The saturated boggy ground will once again be an obstacle before you arrive at the upper reaches. In fact, the name Mosedale is said to derive from the word for mosses and wet ground, and certainly seems appropriate when you're at this point.

You may not see other people on your walk here, but you might well come across some of the native wildlife. Red deer are fairly common on the open hillsides, and molehills will betray the underground excavation of these nocturnal insectivores. Interesting birds include, in spring and summer, ring ouzels on the hillsides, while overhead you may spy buzzards, perhaps a peregrine falcon and, if you're really lucky, England's only golden eagle: this lonely single male has for some years made his home at nearby Haweswater.

Soon, after battling through the mud and water, where the path thins and hides in the long grass, and feeling as though you might just be the only human ever to have undertaken this mission, you'll spy your hard-fought-for destination: the whitewashed shepherd's hut of Mosedale Cottage. Sitting as it does under the now-disused scree slopes of a vast old quarry, some think this building was constructed for the use of the quarry workers during its active years (around 1880–1920). Now its only residents are passing hill-walkers looking for shelter and the occasional shepherd working the land. You'll notice that part of the hut is locked up. This is the shepherd's quarters. But with the building itself offering at least five possible bed chambers, you shouldn't be short of space. There's even a toilet across the courtyard, making this a particularly luxurious bothy in the grand scheme of outdoor shelters.

Enjoy the comfort, but do take a minute to linger before shutting yourself away between your four walls. Few will get to see the stars come out in this lost Lakeland valley, so make sure you take full advantage of being in this wonderfully wild spot.

HERE'S THE PLAN
DAY 1

1 Leaving the last available parking area, turn right onto the road heading southwest. This first tarmac part of the path can be a little tedious, but persevere, past the several farm houses and outbuildings, and through the big metal gates until, finally, you reach Swindale Head.

2 At Swindale Head, continue past the house and through the gate where you finally leave the tarmac road. Follow the gravelly track to emerge into the green fields and rolling fells of this little-visited area of Lakeland. The land undulates over some small hillocks, marked by quad bike tracks. Continue on the main one, ignoring all turn-offs, keeping Swindale Beck to your left.

3 At this point the main path peters out a little. Don't be tempted to follow the water. Instead pick out the faint path that takes you quite steeply uphill. This bit can be boggy and muddy, but you will make out the clear route that cuts first southeast until you come to something of a levelling.

4 Now the path is clearer, though still often sodden – particularly after heavy rain. Follow it well above Mosedale Beck, above the ruins of stone houses and sheepfolds, and through gates and fences. Just before

your path merges with a slightly lower one, you'll spy a bridge crossing the beck – a good clue that you're on the right route. Continue, keeping to the higher ground, and soon, as the land from the nearby fell rises to your left, you'll spy the little copse and old wall that surrounds the bothy. To your right are the spoils of a disused quarry. Continue directly to the bothy. The grass and mud path now becomes more of a definite track, which leads you all the way to your night's shelter.

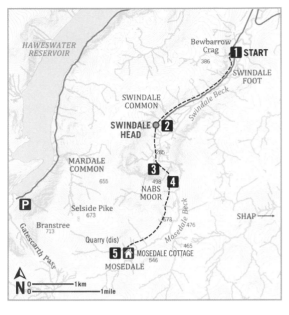

DAY 2

5 In the morning, after having tidied your accommodation and packed up all rubbish, it's time to retrace your steps from the previous night back to your car.

TOP TIP This bothy is occasionally used by shepherds, who may bolt the door once it gets late. Respect their privacy and camp instead: there is lots of dry and flat ground for a pitch within the walled-off cottage courtyard.

NUTS AND BOLTS

PRE-TRIP There is nowhere to pick up supplies at the car park where you begin the walk-in. Instead, make a stop at Penrith *en route* to pick up anything you need. You will also find plenty of B&B/hotel options there, if required.

PUBLIC TRANSPORT This is another weekend that is tricky by public transport. It's easy enough to get to Penrith, which is well served by coaches and trains, but then the only bus that gets close to the start is the 111 operated by Alba Travel (🐭 www.albatravelcumbria.co.uk), which runs only once a week and has an uncertain future. Check 🐭 www.cumbria.gov.uk for up-to-date info.

WHEN TO GO If you can manage it, then either summer – after a period of dry weather – or winter, when the ground is sufficiently frozen and therefore firm, would be best, as it does get awfully boggy here. There's a big solid-fuel burner in the cottage to keep you warm and dry, which you'll probably want to use no matter what time of the year you arrive.

IF YOU DON'T FANCY THE BOTHY? Directly outside the cottage is some good, flat ground on which to pitch a tent.

SHORT OF TIME? Walking in and out in a day is certainly an option. If you want to cut out the tarmac road – though you will pack in a lot more ascent – you can approach from the Haweswater Reservoir side, taking the bridleway up to Gatescarth Pass and approaching Mosedale from the northeast.

TIME TO SPARE? This empty and less-visited side of the Lakes offers ample opportunity for the adventurous. You could check out the wide plateau of the Shap Fells opposite the bothy, if you're feeling like a challenge, or head southwest after a stay at the cottage to check out the nearby Kentmere fells with a wild camp at Small Water.

MORE INFO
Up-to-date bothy conditions 🐭 www.mountainbothies.org.uk
Lake District 🐭 www.lakedistrict.gov.uk
Local 🐭 www.visitcumbria.com

The view from Red Pike over the Mosedale Valley (Stewart Smith Photography/S)

WHERE	Ennerdale, Lake District
DURATION	1 night, 2 days
START/FINISH	Bowness Knott car park ♀ NY109153
MAPS	OS Landranger (1:50,000) 89; OS Explorer (1:25,000) 4

Over on the far western side of the Lake District something big stirs in the forest. It's not one of the many sheep that line the fells. No, this is an altogether different beast that munches the cud then moves slowly on: it's a Galloway cow. And it's not here by accident: these cattle – one of the world's oldest breeds – are part of a grand scheme to re-wild the Ennerdale Valley.

It was back in Mesolithic times, around 8300BC, that humans first began clearing hills and valleys of trees so that they could graze livestock. Before then, the land here would have been coated in native alder, oak and birch. Fast-forward to World War I and World War II,

6 RETURN OF THE WILD

CAMP IN THE ENNERDALE VALLEY, LAKE DISTRICT, WHERE A PIONEERING CONSERVATION PROJECT IS RETURNING THE LANDSCAPE TO ITS ANCIENT, WILD ORIGINS

and this quiet valley had become planted with conifers, a vital source of fast-growing timber for building aircraft and defences. The demand for this wood continued until the late 1990s, when the Forestry Commission realised that they should focus on conservation and bringing people to enjoy their landscape, rather than it serving a purely utilitarian purpose.

> **IT WAS BACK IN MESOLITHIC TIMES, AROUND 8300BC, THAT HUMANS FIRST BEGAN CLEARING HILLS AND VALLEYS OF TREES**

In 2005, the Forestry Commission joined forces with their fellow landowners, the National Trust and United Utilities, together with Natural England, to form the partnership of Wild Ennerdale. Their mission was to return the valley and fells to something more closely resembling the original wild landscape. Rather than stripping the land of all vestiges of human intervention, however, the process has been more one of careful management and letting the landscape develop naturally.

Light lingers over Ennerdale (Stewart Smith Photography/S)

This has involved a number of initiatives. One has been introducing more native broad-leafed trees and juniper into the conifer plantations so that the spruce is less dominant. The spruces themselves are now no longer uniformly trimmed in military-style ranks, so the lines of trees are beginning to look more higgledy-piggledy. They are also being thinned out where possible, and clear-felled areas are not being replanted. Another initiative has been introducing the Galloway cattle, in order to establish a more random grazing regime. Sheep – which graze like lawnmowers, hoovering up whatever comes into their pathway – were removed where possible to make way for these bigger beasts.

Another important element has been modifying the way that the River Liza cuts through the valley floor. Before, intervention was needed in order to control its course and stop it from eroding the footpaths on the riverbanks. Now it's allowed to meander wherever it wants.

And the river is not the only thing allowed to meander. Speak to the rangers and they will actively encourage you to leave the forestry tracks – and all paths, if you want – to pick your own way and embrace the wilderness. And, as long as you do things properly, they are also happy to turn a blind eye to wild camping. This makes Ennerdale the perfect place to enjoy a wild weekend.

In such a wild place you'd expect there to be an abundance of wildlife – apart from the Galloways – and so there is. Birdlife includes goosanders and

common sandpipers on the lake, and pied flycatchers and redstarts in the native forest, while among the mammals are roe deer and red squirrels. If you're very lucky, you may even spot a pine marten – this elusive predator has been seen only a handful of times over the last 20 years, so do report any sightings. In summer, a fine variety of butterflies includes rare marsh fritillaries.

This is a long-term project, so don't expect to see dramatic changes from one week to the next. Instead, keep your eyes open for subtle clues in the landscape that reveal how, under the eye of its human custodians, Ennerdale is slowly freeing itself from its shackles and becoming wild once more.

HERE'S THE PLAN
DAY 1

1 From the car park, take the path that heads southeast along the edge of Ennerdale Water. Follow it under cover of the mix of native and re-wilded trees until you reach a bridge over the water.

2 Unless really pressed for time, take the bridge to the south side of the River Liza and make your way – either on the more defined forestry track or on the more exploratory footpath (which is sometimes swallowed up by the river, which now chooses its own course through the landscape) – towards Black Sail Hut. Trace the river through the trees, getting glimpses every now and again of Pillar and the iconic Pillar Rock, until you reach the third bridge.

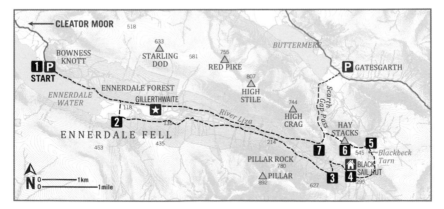

A Marsh fritillary (Henrik Larsson/S)
◀ Looking down into Ennerdale (to the left) from the summit of Haystacks.

3 Cross the third bridge back onto the north bank of the river. Then take the track northwest to meet the one that leads to the most remote YHA hostel in England. Turn right and in less than 500m you'll arrive at Black Sail Hut. This is a good place to refuel – they have some handy benches outside – before continuing up the valley.

4 Make your way along the side of the river (not crossing to the other bank), following the path as it climbs steeply uphill. You'll eventually reach a fence line, which you can cross using a stile. On the other side you'll soon find yourself at Blackbeck Tarn, the perfect wild camp spot for the night.

DAY 2

5 In the morning, pick up the path that leads from the northern end of the tarn southwest then northwest to the summit of Hay Stacks. The views from here down into the Ennerdale Valley, where you've come from, and to the Buttermere Valley, above which you slept, are worth lingering over.

6 Once you've had your fill of the view, continue off the summit to pick up the path down into Scarth Gap Pass, the col between Hay Stacks and the summit of Seat. Here take one last look down into beautiful Buttermere and then turn your back on it to head south back towards Ennerdale.

7 Where the path forks you can take the right-hand option to descend steadily down to the main forestry track on the north of the River Liza. Turn right on this track and follow it all the way back to Bowness Knott and your start point.

Pitch-er perfect at Blackbeck Tarn ⌅
TOP Two trees by Ennerdale Water (Kevin Eaves/S) ⌆
BOTTOM Galloway cattle roam in Ennerdale (www.robgrange.com)

TOPTIP Keep a lookout for the impressive Galloway cattle, which now call the Ennerdale Valley home. The haphazard way in which they graze and tramp around the landscape makes them a vital part of this re-wilding project. Don't put yourself at risk. If cattle appear threatening, simply walk (don't run) to find another way around them.

NUTS AND BOLTS

PRE-TRIP There's nothing to be bought at Bowness Knott so make sure you pick up your supplies first. The nearest town is Cleator Moor, but this is very small. You could try the pretty market town of Egremont for basic supplies, but you're more likely to find what you need in Whitehaven (lots of shops and supermarkets). There are two hostels in the forest that are worth trying for different reasons. Low Gillerthwaite Field Centre (👟 www.lgfc.org.uk) offers camping and dorms, plus – at certain times of the year – special Dark Sky events where you get to star gaze with the experts. The other option is the iconic Black Sail Hut (see below).

PUBLIC TRANSPORT The nearest you can get by public transport is Cleator Moor. That's by taking the Stagecoach 33 bus from Whitehaven (every 30 mins), itself reached via train from Carlisle. That still leaves you about 10km from the start point. You could arrange a taxi from there or resign yourself to a long walk-in.

WHEN TO GO This weekend can be enjoyed all year. Part of the route is featured on Wainwright's famous Coast to Coast walk, so on weekends and during the summer holidays it can become a little crowded.

IF YOU DON'T FANCY THE WILD CAMP? A stay at Black Sail Hut (👟 www.yha. org.uk/hostel/black-sail) will be a night to remember. A former shepherd's hut, it offers basic beds and one shared bathroom in a superb location – indeed, this is Britain's most remote YHA hostel. In 2014, it underwent a £250,000 restoration to make it more efficient and sustainable. It's now like a bothy, but with all mod cons and cooked meals available. You should definitely consider a stay here as an alternative to camping, but you will need to book in advance through the website.

SHORT OF TIME? Start from Gatesgarth on the Buttermere side of the fells and nip up to Blackbeck Tarn much more quickly. Bear in mind that in doing this you will miss out the great wild landscape of Ennerdale, although you will have the chance to peer at it from the top of Hay Stacks.

TIME TO SPARE? This is one of the best wild weekends to extend. From adding a night in Black Sail Hut or High Gillerthwaite hostel (and its great astronomy programmes in winter), to tackling the ridge of High Stile, High Crag and Red Pike above the valley for a wild camp with altitude, you could easily spend a week exploring.

MORE INFO
Ennerdale 👟 www.wildennerdale.co.uk
Youth Hostels Association 👟 www.yha.org.uk
Lake District 👟 www.golakes.co.uk; www.lakedistrict.gov.uk; www.ntlakesoutdoors.org.uk

View into Ennerdale towards High Crag and Haystacks (Stewart Smith Photography/S) ➤

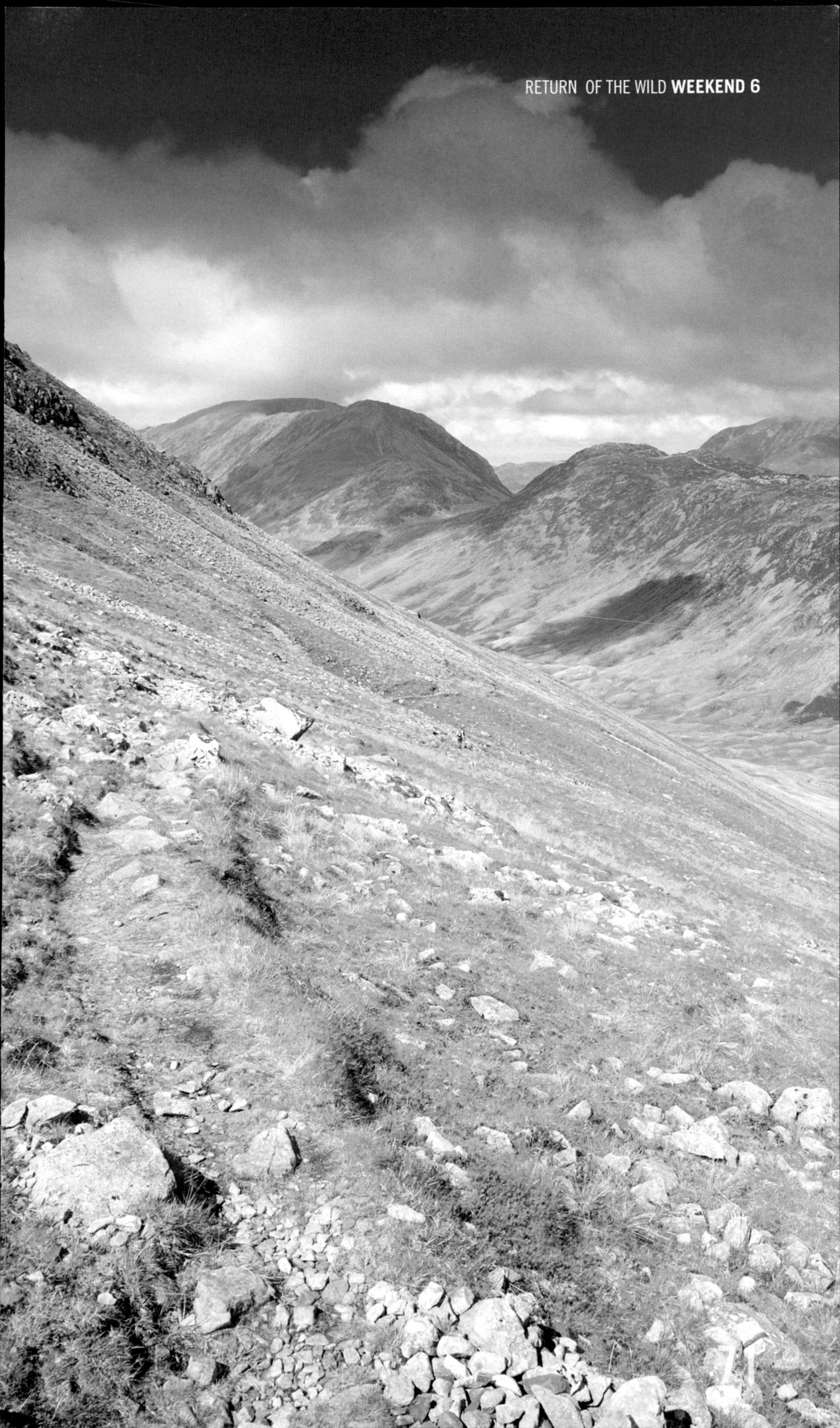

7 CAVE DREAMS

SLEEP IN A MOUNTAIN CAVE
ON DOVE CRAG, THE LAKE DISTRICT

WHERE	Dove Crag, Patterdale, Lake District
DURATION	1 night, 2 days
START/FINISH	Cow Bridge car park ♀ NY402134
MAPS	OS Landranger (1:50,000) 90; OS Explorer (1:25,000) 5

Flick through any geology textbook and you'll quickly discover that, for millennia, our world has been carved, cleaved and chopped up by glaciers, wind and rain – not to mention humankind. These actions have created a network of cracks and overhangs for curious souls to explore. Caves tend to be at the bottom of hills, hidden underground or beneath piles of boulders. But find a cave up high, on the side of a mountain summit, and you'll have found somewhere very special indeed.

Enter Priest's Hole. Hidden high up on the side of a fell called Dove Crag, this is perhaps one of Lakeland's most celebrated natural cavities. Its origins remain a mystery but its current use does not. Upon arrival, you'll feel almost as though you've stumbled into a bothy: there's usually a collection of tarps or groundsheets left by previous users, occasionally some camping stove gas canisters (usually left because there's some gas remaining, rather than simply discarded), and even a plastic box containing a visitors' book, along with a pen so you can record your visit.

> **ON A CLEAR DAY, WHILE SITTING INSIDE, IT'S LIKE HAVING A PENTHOUSE VIEW OVER THE NORTHERN LAKE DISTRICT**

Sleeping in Priest's Hole is almost a right of passage for outdoor aficionados, even though many who talk about it have never actually spent the night. But there's no reason why you can't: this isn't a dark, scary tunnel so deep into the mountainside that you'll feel it's swallowed you up; it's merely a shallow overhang, big enough to keep the wind and rain at bay, but open enough to prevent any claustrophobia. On a clear day, while sitting inside, it's like having a penthouse view over the northern Lake District. The open side offers a 180-degree panoramic window, affording a real-life vista so clear you'd swear you were looking at a high-definition image.

Staying in the caves of Lakeland is nothing new. One of Britain's most famous cave-dwellers lived in Borrowdale in the 1930s, tucked into the lower slopes of Castle Crag. His name was Millican Dalton, and he was no tramp – condemned by hard times to sleeping rough – but had made the move by choice, quitting a good job and conventional life in London.

Sporting a Tyrolean hat, long beard and often with a Woodbine clamped between his lips, Millican even made many of his own clothes – which, some suggest, were a precursor for some of today's lightweight kit. He would earn a little money by taking groups of men and women out climbing, walking and camping. Such behaviour was taboo at the time, but that didn't bother this pacifist, teetotal vegetarian. He would famously brag about his split-level cave home, which even had a ready water source in the form of a stream running through it. Today you can still see the words he inscribed onto the wall: 'Don't waste words jump to conclusions.'

Sadly Millican is now gone, but his legacy and thirst for adventure can live on in all of us. There is no better way to honour one of Lakeland's finest than finding our own cave, high above the Patterdale Valley, and spending a night in the great outdoors.

HERE'S THE PLAN
DAY 1

1 Leaving the car park via the gate in the southwest corner, follow the wide track where it passes under trees on the edge of Brothers Water. This is clear and easy to follow until you reach the farm at Hartsop Hall.

2 Once at the farm, walk past the buildings and you will see the path fork. Take the fainter track on the far right, which begins to climb uphill. Things can get muddy at this point. Follow it above the wall line and over some very old stiles and ruined gates, climbing as you go. The trees eventually give way to open fellside and you then meet the water of Dovedale Beck.

3 Don't cross the bridge to the beck's southern bank, but keep the beck to your left and continue along the path. The track begins to climb over rocks and boulders, and you'll note the spoil of old buildings to

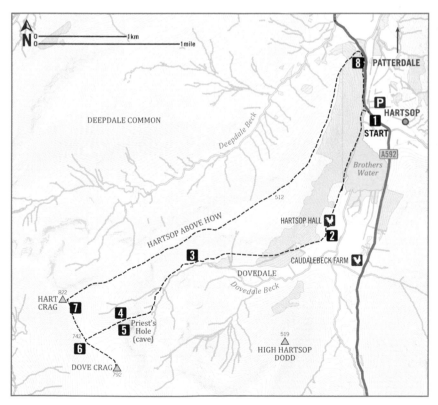

your right. It's around this point that, looking uphill in clear conditions, you'll get your first glimpse of the cave to which you're heading: it appears as a dark, egg-shaped shadow near the top of the crag and just right of centre. The path steepens considerably here until the ground begins to level out and becomes grassier. You should see a large boulder ahead: walk to this.

4 Look left from the boulder and you should be able to make out a rough path – almost like a sheep track – that curves up and around the side of the rocks to the left. Head for that, towards the rocks in front of you. You'll need to use your hands in a couple of places, but it gets no more technical than that. After about five minutes you should find yourself at the entrance to Priest's Hole, your room for the night.

Priest's Hole, visible from a distance ⋏

DAY 2

5 After remembering to fill in the visitors' book – and taking out any excess rubbish you can carry – carefully retrace your steps back down to the big boulder you left yesterday. If you're in a rush you can simply return to the car, following the same route you took up. If you have time, however, continue uphill to the col between the peaks of Dove Crag and Hart Crag.

6 Wainwright baggers will probably first want to nip southeast to summit the mountain inside which they have just camped. From there, you can retrace your steps to the col and then continue for a final push up to the summit of Hart Crag.

7 From Hart Crag take the obvious track northeast that follows the ridge along Hartsop Above How. This path steadily loses height then drops to the north of Low Wood.

8 Turn onto the road and walk back the short distance to Cow Bridge and your start point.

> **TOP TIP** Caves are naturally damp places and Priest's Hole has a very wide opening. Make sure you take a waterproof bivvy for your sleeping bag, plenty of warm layers, hot food and drink, and consider bringing a piece of tarp to lay under your camping mat as the floor is rocky and sharp in places. As always, take out all rubbish with you.

Enjoying the view from Lakeland's best cave sleep

NUTS AND BOLTS

PRE-TRIP Once in the cave it's unlikely you'll want to keep climbing up and down to fetch water, so take a good supply. If you do need more, fetch it as soon as you arrive, when it's still daylight, so that you're sure of finding the cave again. The nearest shop is the small store in Patterdale (🌐 www.patterdalevillagestore.co.uk), which sells some food and drink. For more in the way of camping supplies, head to either Windermere/Ambleside (south) or Keswick/Penrith (north) before you set off.

PUBLIC TRANSPORT The nearest you can get to the start of your adventure using public transport is the Patterdale Hotel, around 5km from the start. Take the Stagecoach Bus 108 (one every four hours) from Penrith, which is well served both by buses and National Rail. You can walk or get a taxi from Patterdale to the start.

WHEN TO GO Winter may be too cold to sleep in a cave at this height. Be careful on the rocks at other times, especially after rain or when it's frosty.

IF YOU DON'T FANCY THE CAVE? There are numerous points *en route* to pitch a tent. The flatter, grassy section below the cave is one such site, and also near to a water source, so makes a great plan B if the cave is full.

SHORT OF TIME? Cut your return route by retracing your steps from day 1, but this time crossing the bridge over Dove Beck to take you to the south side. Follow the path all the way down to Hartsop Hall and beyond. You can, if you prefer, visit the cave as a day walk rather than an overnight stop.

TIME TO SPARE? There are lots more wild camping options around here, from summit pitches to a hammock sleep in the woods – or, simply, a tarnside stay at Brothers Water. Get out your OS map and start planning.

MORE INFO

Lake District 🌐 www.lakedistrict.gov.uk
Millican Dalton 📖 *Millican Dalton: A Search for Romance and Freedom* by Matthew David Entwistle, Mountainmere Research, 2004
Patterdale 🌐 www.patterdaletoday.co.uk

Common buzzard (BogdanBoev/S) 🔺
View towards Brothers Water (Richard Bowden/S) ➤

WHERE	Byrness, Northumberland
DURATION	1 night, 2 days
START/FINISH	Byrness car park (near to recycle bins) ♥ NT770024
MAPS	OS Landranger (1:50,000) 80; OS Explorer (1:25,000) 16

Way up in the far northern reaches of England, before the land morphs seamlessly into Scotland, lies the least populated national park in the UK: Northumberland. Not only do fewer people live within its boundaries than in any other park, but – and perhaps even better – fewer people visit it. But they really should. Encompassing both the bare, rolling peaks of the Cheviots and the tree-covered summits around Kielder Forest, it's an atmospheric expanse of wilderness covering all types of terrain.

As is often the way in wilder areas, Byrness is home to some great folklore. Northumbrian legend has it that Simonside Dwarfs, known as

8 BEWARE THE DUERGAR

HIKE THROUGH THE REMOTE CHEVIOTS ON THE TRAIL OF MALEVOLENT DWARVES IN BYRNESS, NORTHUMBERLAND NATIONAL PARK

Duergar (an Old Norse word for dwarf) lurk on the hills, especially at night. These ugly and malicious troublemakers are there – supposedly – to lead walkers astray, often carrying torches to guide the unwary into one of the many bogs. Come dawn, however, these mischievous little beings reputedly disappear, so all you have to do is see out the night.

What better way to spot a duergar than by taking a walk up onto some of these distinctively rounded Cheviot Hills? Up here, a network of national trails and old cattle drover routes will lead you safely back, even if the duergar do come out to play. You'll begin with an ascent along the Pennine Way, the most famous of all the UK's long-

> **" IT'S AN ATMOSPHERIC EXPANSE OF WILDERNESS COVERING ALL TYPES OF TERRAIN "**

distance paths, which passes through Northumberland *en route* from the Derbyshire peaks to the Scottish borders. Following it up and along the ridge of Ravens Pike, you'll encounter few other long-distance walkers,

Spithope bothy nestles among the Cheviots

as many choose to cut out this long and exposed section entirely, judging it 'too wild'. You'll also be treading a fine line between Scotland and England, as part of this path follows the Border Ridge, between the two.

The rounded bumps of the Cheviots may not, on first glance, look that wild to you, but clearly the army thinks they are. The Ministry of Defence's Otterburn Army Training Estate frequently uses the area just right of the Pennine Way to practise manoeuvres and test its artillery. It's not uncommon to hear distant gunfire as you navigate here, adding an altogether different element of wildness to your walk.

But fear not: away from mythical dwarfs and the military comes a perfect finale to this foray into Northumberland's wilderness. You can end the day in the safety of Spithope, one of the cosiest bothies there is. Perched a little way down the valley, this stone shelter comes complete with an easy water source on its doorstep, comfy bunk beds that surround a very efficient fuel-burning stove, and even something of its own garden – guaranteed duergar-free. From here you can watch the sun set over the forest, glad that this really is the least visited national park because now you can enjoy a night like this with nobody there but yourself. And the duergar, of course.

HERE'S THE PLAN
DAY 1

1 From the parking places up near the recycle bins take the signposted Pennine Way through the gate. Continue through the field, alongside the adjacent property's fence, then through the kissing gate. A bridleway marked on the map to your left at this point is ridiculously overgrown and rarely walked so, unless you are eager to crack on to the bothy, continue along the Pennine Way, heading uphill first then down to cross a forestry track. You'll begin to climb once more, crossing a couple more tracks until, eventually, the trees give way to the clear ground of Byrness Hill summit.

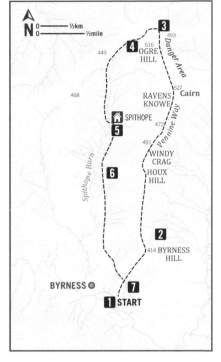

2 After enjoying the views, begin your undulating trail over the tops of Houx Hill, Windy Crag and Raven's Knowe, keeping your eyes out for the elusive duergar as you follow the Pennine Way.

3 Just past the summit of Ogre Hill, leave the Pennine Way to pick up the path that heads downhill southwest. Soon you will join a forestry track at a bend.

4 Take the path to your right and follow it for a little over 2km. You'll soon spy the bridge that takes you over Spithope Burn, with the bothy a little uphill on the other side. Cross the bridge to reach your shelter for the night.

DAY 2

5 A public bridleway runs from the bothy on the east side of the burn and rejoins the forestry track you crossed at the start of the walk. This is the route described here, and is the preferred way for walkers due to forestry

83

TOP TIP On leaving the bothy, if you're finding the official route on the bridleway too tricky or the weather is very bad, it's better to take the bridge over Spithope Burn from the night before and turn left onto the forestry track. You can then follow this – being careful to avoid any forestry vehicles – all the way to the main road, where you turn left to complete the walk back (just over 1km) to the turn off-for your car. It's a bit of a trudge but a sensible plan B.

traffic elsewhere. Take care, however, as the path can be tricky to find due to recent felling, with felled trees and hidden watercourses underfoot. Use walking poles and do not be afraid to take the more obvious, alternative route (see *Top Tip*, above).

From the bothy, head down towards the smaller stream that feeds into Spithope Burn and cross it using the stepping stones. You'll see a faint path. (NB: the bridleway marked on the map does not follow the true course now on the ground.) Follow this path uphill then pick your way carefully through the long grass and felled wood. You'll see a fence line to your right, which you can use as a navigational marker, keeping it on your right as you head uphill. When the fence bends to the right (it forms a large rectangle), start to cut across to it; you may find one of the Public Footpath signs hidden in the undergrowth. Once above the fence line and the massive rectangular enclosure it forms, continue, keeping the fence to your right once more. The path should now be bearing south slightly downhill and undulating. Keep going and you'll soon reach the wider remains of an old forestry track, covered in long grass but much firmer underfoot. Continue a little further until the grass subsides and you're finally back on a proper forestry track.

6 The wildest section of the journey now over, simply follow the track for about 2.5km ignoring all turn-offs – which are very overgrown, anyway – until you reach the familiar sight of the Pennine Way footpath crossing your track.

7 This time turn right onto the Pennine Way, first climbing uphill then descending again into the forest and back to the kissing gate. Follow the path through the field and back through the final gate, before emerging into the parking area near the hotel and recycle bins where you started.

NUTS AND BOLTS

PRE-TRIP There is little in the village of Byrness other than a hostel, hotel and restaurant, so get any supplies you need before you head out there. The nearest towns are Hexham (south) or Hawick (north).

PUBLIC TRANSPORT National Express coaches ( www.nationalexpress.com) stop at Byrness. There's a local bus to Byrness from Jedburgh, line 131 (www.roadhoggs.net), which you can reach using buses from Hawick and Carlisle, but the service is infrequent. There's also a very limited service from Hexham on the 883 with Howard Snaith (www.howardsnaith.co.uk), though this runs only three times per week.

WHEN TO GO The hills in this area are great to visit year-round, as is the bothy. The rough track and felled trees on the way back from the Spithope can become slippery and hazardous, though, so it's best to visit after a period of dry weather.

IF YOU DON'T FANCY THE BOTHY? There's a small, flat area outside the building, surrounded by a stone wall, which would make a perfect wild camp spot if the bothy is full or you don't fancy being inside.

SHORT OF TIME? Getting to and from the bothy can be done reasonably fast if you stick to the lower forestry track/bridleway, following a straightforward in-and-out route, and leave out the hills above.

TIME TO SPARE? If you're feeling fresh you could walk further along the Pennine Way, taking in the wilder landscape further north or heading through more forest to the south. Remember that the military do sometimes train with firearms in the area east of Windy Crag and Ogre Hill, so check before you go exploring off-track that it's safe to do so. Call ahead, look out for signs and flags, and obey any instructions.

MORE INFO
Up-to-date bothy conditions www.mountainbothies.org.uk
Military Range Liaison Officer ☎ +44 (0)191 239 4201 or +44 (0)191 239 4227;
 www.gov.uk/government/publications/otterburn-firing-times
Local www.visitnorthumberland.com
National Park www.northumberlandnationalpark.org.uk

The curlew is the emblem of Northumberland National Park (Erni/S)
Just follow the signposts to the Pennine Way (Jeanie333/S)

WHEN COMING TO WILD PLACES
IT'S NICE TO KNOW THAT
THEY ARE NEVER REALLY OURS:
WE MERELY BORROW
THEM FOR A WHILE

WALES

9 POETRY AND MADNESS

SPEND A NIGHT AMID MYTHS AND LEGENDS ON THE SUMMIT OF CADAIR IDRIS, MID WALES

WHERE	Cadair Idris, Mid Wales
DURATION	1 night, 2 days
START/FINISH	Minffordd car park **Q** SH732115
MAPS	OS Landranger (1:50,000) 124; OS Explorer (1:25,000) 23

any mountains have spawned legends: Snowdon has its Arthurian connections (legend has it King Arthur is buried there), while Scotland's Ben Macdui is often cited as the home of the ghostly 'grey man'. But no legend is quite so ominous as those that surround Cadair Idris. According to folklore, anybody who attempts to stay a night on the summit of this, the most popular mountain in Wales after its highest peak, will either go mad, become a poet or – the most alarming – die.

In my experience, two of these postulations seem reasonable. A stroll up to the craggy summit, skirting the huge glacial cirque that holds a mammoth lake and offers some of the most breathtaking views of southern Snowdonia, could certainly bring out the poet in even the most prosaic of visitors. Equally, the stretch of the walk between Craig Cwm Amarch and the summit of Penygadair (the moniker given to Cadair Idris's 893m top), which seems to continue endlessly before it

> **"**
> **THESE ARE SCRATCHES GOUGED INTO THE BEDROCK DURING THE LAST ICE AGE**
> **"**

suddenly deposits you safely at the trig point, is enough to make you question your route-finding skills and leave you feeling as though you might actually have gone insane. But dying just by spending the night there? Perhaps only in that the views you'll be rewarded with when you wake up on the summit the next morning – with the Mawddach estuary, the serrated peaks of northern Snowdonia and the rolling undulations of mid Wales to the south – might make you feel as though you have passed on to somewhere more heavenly.

Brave this adventure and you'll get to decide for yourself, as not only will you have the chance to take on one of the most daring summit sleeps in Wales, but also to admire the many Arctic-alpine plants that abound on the higher slopes, from dwarf willow to the bright sprays of purple saxifrage. Lower down, keep your eyes peeled for bilberry, heather and a variety of mosses. And, as you're scrambling over the rocks circling the cwm, look out for the many glacial striations. These are scratches gouged into the bedrock during the last ice age: the time when Llyn Cau was formed.

This lake is steeped in further legends – quite apart from the trio of possible fates that might befall a summit-sleeper. Standing on the shore of Llyn Cau, it's easy to understand how Cadair Idris – which means 'Chair of Idris' – got its name. According to local lore, Idris was a giant who would sit here and gaze at the stars in the night sky. And looking at how the mountain rises around the back and side of the lake to form an amphitheatre of steep slopes and scree, it's easy to see the resemblance to a giant chair – or, more correctly, a giant's chair.

Up at the summit you'll find an emergency shelter. Another local tale from bygone days concerns a man from Abergynolwyn or Dolgellau (it depends upon who you ask), who every day in summer would hike up with his pony to sell walkers sandwiches and lemonade from this hut. It's said that this is where the so-called 'Pony Path' gets its name. Sadly, you'll now have to bring up your own refreshments. And bear in mind, before loading up, that you should be taking a tent rather than relying on the draughty stone refuge.

Oh, and there is one final legend you should know about. Celtic mythology tells us that this is the roaming place of Gwyn ap Nudd, aka Lord of the Underworld. He is said to patrol this peak with his pack of hounds. But don't worry: you'll only hear the howls if he's about to come and take you. Otherwise, I'm sure that distant barking is nothing more than a over-excited Jack Russell...

Stile *en route* to Cadair Idris (BMJ/S)

HERE'S THE PLAN
DAY 1

1 Leave the car park via the gate in the corner by the toilets and turn right onto the path. Follow this down to the café (seasonal opening times) and turn left past it. Soon you'll see a gate and a sign on your right. Go through this to start on the Minffordd Path.

2 Climbing steadily, you'll first be under the cover of trees, weaving around stones on a well-maintained, though often muddy, path. You rise fast, so it's a knee-acher, but you'll soon emerge alongside Nant Cadair, a large river.

3 Don't take the footbridge on your right, but note it for your return journey. Continue on the path ahead, keeping the water to your right, and you will steadily make the climb up to Llyn Cau.

4 The path begins to swing uphill here, bearing south. But don't rush off without taking a minute to wander over to the lake, surrounded on three sides by its rocky guardians. It is breathtakingly beautiful, and a good camping option if you either arrive late on a Friday evening or want to stay for two nights. Retrace your steps to the Minffordd Path and follow it up, through the rocks. It won't be long before you reach the summit ridge, where the upper circuit of the lake begins. Follow the path as it traces the southern end of Llyn Cau, undulating as it goes, before swinging northeast where it reaches a fence line and a cairn.

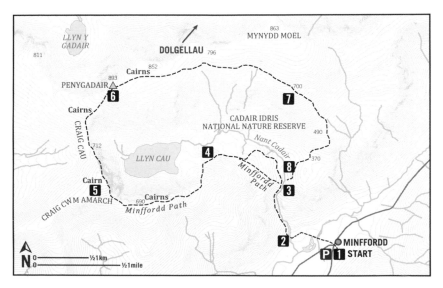

5 Continue on the path, now heading resolutely northeast along Craig Cau. You'll see where the alternative, very loose, scrambly route up the mountain (not recommended) meets your path on your right. Soon after this you'll meet your final climb, littered with many a pile of stones marking the route. Before long you'll top out on the summit of Penygadair. Here, as well as the trig point, there's also an old hut that can serve as an emergency shelter. Hopefully you will have planned this trip for a clear, wind-free night and, of course, brought your tent. Immediately outside the hut, looking down on Llyn y Gadair, there is a flat, fairly stone-free section of land that is perfect for pitching. If it's windy you could descend a little either southeast or northwest for more shelter.

DAY 2

6 After enjoying the world-class views from just beyond your tent flap, continue on the path northwest. This is mainly on grassy ground, with some rocks. Although the map shows one path that sticks religiously to the summit ridge, you will find a lower option about 500m after you leave the summit by taking the right-hand (lower) path where it forks. If summit ticks are not important, or the weather has turned, this cuts out the ascent/reascent to Mynydd Moel and slowly descends over rough and rocky ground. You'll also get some great views back over the route you've taken, as this path takes you nearer the edges of the ridge.

7 You'll come to a stone wall with a stile. Cross this and follow the wall down, keeping it to your right. After just over 500m the path turns west, descending further, then turns more to the south, leading you down to the river and the bridge that you saw on your way up.

8 Cross the footbridge over the Nant Cadair and retrace your steps down to the café and car park.

Looking back to Cadair Idris from just before step 7

NUTS AND BOLTS

PRE-TRIP Dolgellau is the place to find supplies in advance. There's a well-stocked Co-op and a camping store, although in my experience the latter doesn't often offer camping meals or gas, so best to stock up before you arrive. You will find a couple of B&B options here as well as pubs offering evening meals.

PUBLIC TRANSPORT The only way to get to the start of this particular route is by taxi. You can take buses as far as Dolgellau from the North Wales coast (Express Motors line X1; 🖱 www.expressmotors.co.uk) or from Ruabon train station (GHA Coaches; 🖱 www.ghacoaches.co.uk). Buses also connect Dolgellau with the train stations at Fairbourne (Lloyds Coaches, three times/day) or Machynlleth (Lloyds Coaches/Express Motors, every hour).

WHEN TO GO Cadair Idris is a spectacular mountain all year, although come the winter snows, an ice axe, crampons and the ability to use them correctly are essential. Summer is busy but, with good weather, makes for a memorable weekend. Spring and autumn are usually less crowded, providing you don't come on a bank holiday weekend — or Easter!

IF YOU DON'T FANCY THE SUMMIT CAMP? The hut on the summit is meant as an emergency shelter so you shouldn't plan to stay there unless desperate. If the weather is bad, consider sleeping lower down from the top instead.

SHORT OF TIME? The route described here can also be done as a full day's walk, though it's a long one, so start early.

TIME TO SPARE? To really get under the skin of the mountain, stay an extra night — with a sleep next to Llyn Cau as well as on the summit.

MORE INFO
Cadair Idris 🖱 www.ccgc.gov.uk
Snowdonia 🖱 www.eryri-npa.gov.uk
Local 🖱 www.discoverdolgellau.com

Cadair Idris: a tent's eye view ⋀
Stile *en route* to Cadair Idris (Ian Keirle/D) ➢

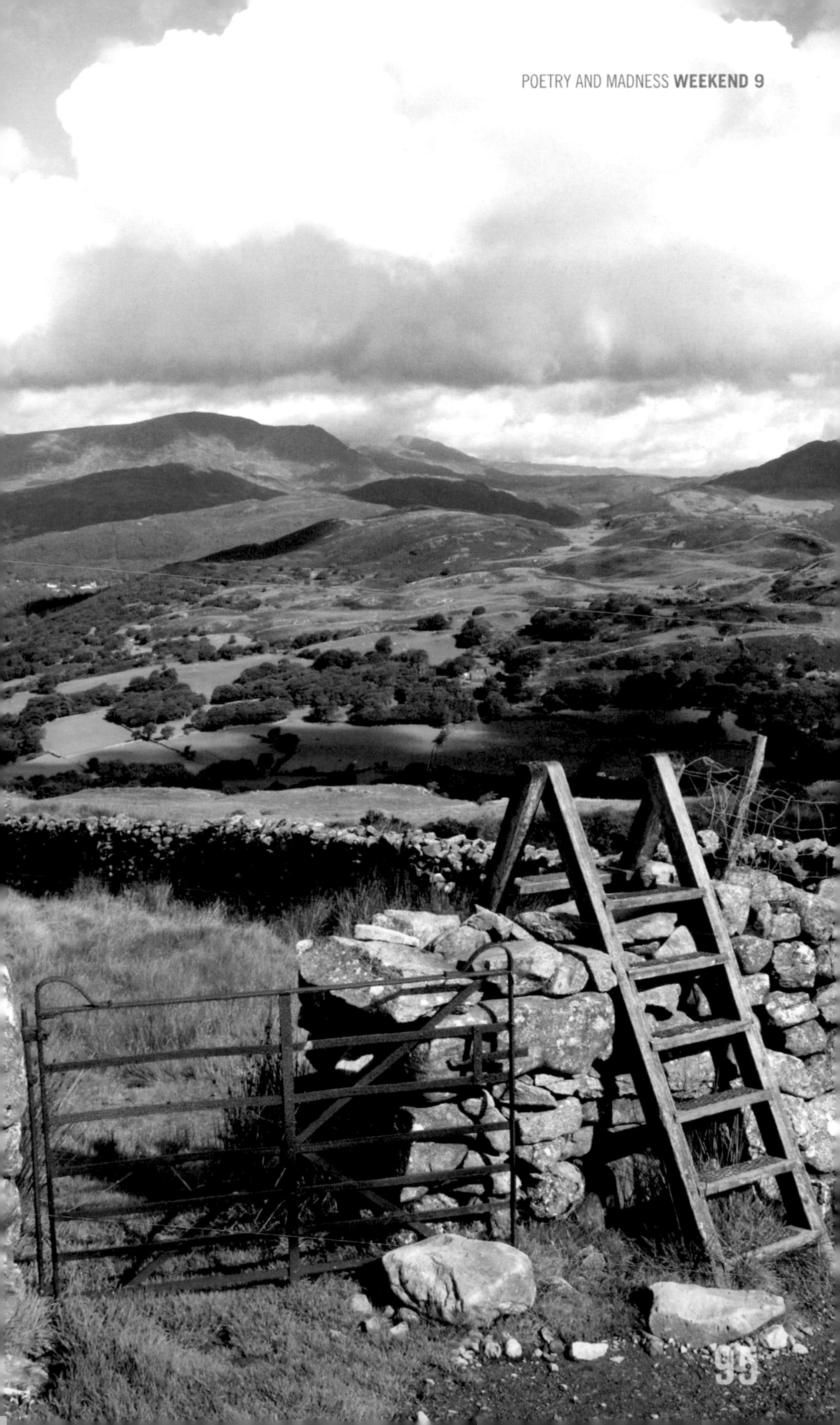

WHERE	Croesor, North Wales
DURATION	1 night, 2 days
START/FINISH	Croesor car park ♥ SH631446
MAPS	OS Landranger (1:50,000) 115; OS Explorer (1:25,000) 17, 18

I t's rare you'll find a hotel slap bang in the middle of the mountains – and even rarer that it will boast four stars. But that's exactly what you'll discover near the foot of a peak called Cnicht in North Wales. OK, so maybe the star rating isn't exactly official, and perhaps the beds are a little harder than you might hope and the bathroom more… al fresco. But still, if stars were awarded for location alone, the night's accommodation that awaits you on this escapade would easily merit a confident five.

Tucked in between the boulders above an unnamed lake is a collection of rocks that make up a stone hotel – or, to be more accurate, a cosy chamber

10 CONQUER THE WELSH MATTERHORN

SLEEP IN A CAVE ON THE SIDE OF A JAGGED MOUNTAIN PEAK, CNICHT, NORTH WALES

that comfortably accommodates one or two people. Rugged it may be, but the view over towards what some call the Matterhorn of Wales more than makes up for it.

Ah, the ubiquitous Matterhorn! It seems every country in the world has one: a dramatic, jagged peak that takes your breath away. Cnicht is no exception, when viewed from the southwest it does – if you squint hard and allow a healthy

> **" IF STARS WERE AWARDED FOR LOCATION ALONE, THE NIGHT'S ACCOMMODATION THAT AWAITS YOU ON THIS ESCAPADE WOULD EASILY MERIT A CONFIDENT FIVE "**

dose of imagination – look very similar to its Swiss *doppelgänger*. The mountain's name is thought to come from an old English word for knight – though with the 'K' in this case voiced – as its shape also resembles that of a knight's helmet, and it certainly looks cavalier.

Though Cnicht might not have the altitude or the allure of the real Matterhorn, it has definitely made an impression on the locals. On arrival

Cnicht: small but perfectly formed (Gail Johnson/S)

97

at the car park in the village of Croesor you'll see the collection of slates that have been lovingly decorated by the local schoolchildren, nearly every one showing the mountain in some way. Like a wise village elder, the peak watches proudly over its young.

Once a huge quarrying area, with workers living on the lower flanks – their spoils are visible from the walk to your rocky hotel – the village's population has shrunk since that enterprise died. But a strong community spirit still remains. As recently as 2011, when a big corporation was set to buy one of the farms and turn it into a hotel, the locals clubbed together and transformed it into a café, bunkhouse and art gallery, lovingly curated for the visitors who come to admire their towering guardian. A walk to the summit when you visit the area is practically mandatory – and, as it's only a little over 500m, it's not long before you're soon reaping the rewards. From the top of this glaciated U-shaped valley are views over the River Glasglyn, out to Cardigan Bay and beyond. And after taking in the landscape there's no better way to feel a part of it than to sleep in its bosom, in your very own cave hotel. Here you're assured of no unwelcome early wake-up calls – except for the creeping sunlight at dawn; no noisy neighbours – unless you count the shrill cry of a peregrine falcon overhead; and, definitely, no hefty bill on check out.

Looking east from Cnicht ⤒
Peregrine falcon in dashing pursuit of prey (Robert L Kothenbeutel/S) ◄

HERE'S THE PLAN
DAY 1

1 As you exit the car park, turn right to follow the minor road uphill. Take a minute to enjoy the slate spikes in the ground (on your right after you pass the car park), decorated with pictures by children from the local school – most with Cnicht as their theme. Carry on through the gate, the going becoming steeper under the trees, until the path splits into two.

2 Turn right to pass through the gate and onto the main track up Cnicht (not marked on the OS map but very clear on the ground). It's steady going at first, as you tick off the contour lines, with small rocky outcrops protruding from the otherwise smooth grass as though trying to compete with the peak itself.

3 A rather odd section of level ground – known by some as 'the football pitch' – opens before you here. Walk over to the spiky rocks on your left. From this point you can see down to the small lake and the cave where you'll be heading for the night. The path now becomes a little scrambly – nothing too challenging but you will need to use your hands at times. Continue heading up, gaining height more quickly now. Soon you'll find yourself on the summit of Cnicht.

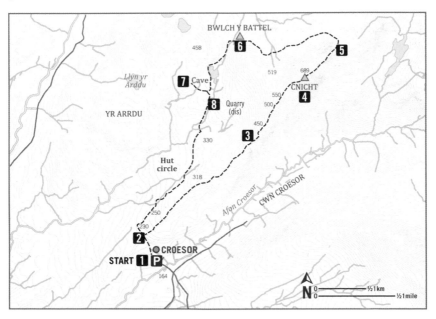

4 Congratulations! You've conquered the Welsh Matterhorn – and no supplementary oxygen, months of training or qualified guide were required! Enjoy the views then continue along the ridge for about 500m. Where the path drops to a fairly flat section, make your break downhill to the west.

5 Be careful; rabbit holes are hidden by long grass on this off-piste route. There is no path – you'll be following sheep tracks – so assess the terrain carefully to plan your way forward. You want to head roughly west to reach Bwlch y Battel.

6 From Bwlch y Battel descend towards the lake, bearing southwest where a faint path begins to appear. Follow this to the water and then cut around its edge, on the west side. Up to your right you will see a boulder field. Your cave is in here, made up of fallen slabs. Look out for the chalk inscription, where someone has scribbled '4* Hotel' (and more recently 'Heartbreak Hotel'). This is your bed for the night.

TOP TIP The cave sleeps one person comfortably and two, if you're friends. Any more than that is a bit tight. Be prepared with a tent or bivvy in case someone has beaten you to it.

DAY 2

7 Leaving the comfort of your cave head downhill, southwest, towards the rocky slope in front of you. Almost immediately you will pick up a path. Follow it as you edge alongside the stream, losing height as you go. You'll soon need to cross this stream (it's not wide) and head for the rocks where the path contours around them.

8 Don't be tempted to turn at the wall line and head towards Cnicht again. Instead, continue on your grassy, often boggy, path, heading south then southwest. You'll pass through a couple of gates as you start to make your way back towards the path you used for your ascent. The easiest option is to join this and retrace your steps to the start.

Spoils from quarrying remain all over Snowdonia. (Gail Johnson/S)
Room with a view: the cave near Cnicht.

NUTS AND BOLTS

PRE-TRIP Croesor is a lovely village but not the place for camping supplies. The nearest town for these is either Porthmadog (if coming from the coast), Beddgelert (small, but close for emergency food/drink), Blaenau Ffestiniog or Betws-y-Coed. In the summer of 2014 the community-run café (Oriel Caffi Croesor) announced it would be closing but hoped to reopen at a later date, along with a bunkhouse. Check for an update before you set off. There is a portaloo in the car park.

PUBLIC TRANSPORT Unfortunately this route is impossible to do using public transport. The nearest you can get to the start is by taking the train to Blaenau Ffestiniog then a taxi up to the village, about 6km away.

WHEN TO GO Cnicht is a fantastic little peak at any time of year. For a cave sleep, however, spring or summer is best, as it can get very cold in autumn and winter. Take plenty of warm layers whenever you go.

IF YOU DON'T FANCY THE CAVE HOTEL? The tarn you pass *en route* is a great place to pitch. The ground can be a little saturated, so move a little further away to where it is firmer underfoot. With a bivvy, you could also sleep outside the cave, although the ground is sloping.

SHORT OF TIME? The whole circuit can be walked in a day. For something shorter still you could just walk to the cave: the perfect place for an al fresco lunch.

TIME TO SPARE? You could start with the cave sleep and do the walk in reverse up to the summit, then instead of descending, head further along the ridge to complete a horseshoe over to Llyn Cwm Corsiog and Llyn Croesor, with a wild camp on the way. Then return to your start.

MORE INFO
Snowdonia ‡ www.visitsnowdonia.info
Walking ‡ www.eryri-npa.gov.uk
Local ‡ www.blaenauffestiniog.org

The 'football pitch' on Cnicht

11 ALIEN EXPLORATIONS

ON THE TRAIL OF MYTHS ANCIENT AND
MODERN IN THE BERWYN MOUNTAINS, MID WALES

WHERE	Berwyn Mountains Mid Wales
DURATION	1 night, 2 days
START/FINISH	Tan y Pistyll car park ♥ SJ076294
MAPS	OS Landranger (1:50,000) 125; OS Explorer (1:25,000) 255

You've probably heard the story of Roswell, the legendary 'cover-up' of an alien spaceship that supposedly crashed in the small New Mexico town. But you may not realise that Wales has its own extra-terrestrial tale, which took place in the folds of the Berwyn Mountains. Rising skyward amid a cluster of small Welsh villages, these unassuming hills, punctuated with waterfalls, lakes and quagmires, were – back on 23 January 1974 – the alleged landing site of little green men.

The story goes that at around 20.30, villagers in Llandrillo, Bala and Llanderfel heard a sudden explosion that shook their houses, furniture and belongings. Various residents had reported seeing streams of light just before the explosion, prompting local nurse Pat Evans to race up the mountain to help out at what she feared would be an aircraft crash. When she got there, instead of wreckage all she saw were strange orbs of bright light, surrounded by smaller glows. Realising she couldn't get close enough to investigate further, and assuming no help was required, she began to return home – only to be stopped by the military and ordered away. In the days that followed villagers were questioned by a number of mysterious 'men in black', and army vehicles were said to have packed the B roads of this tiny township, keeping their mission hush-hush.

> **WALES HAS ITS OWN EXTRA-TERRESTRIAL TALE, WHICH TOOK PLACE IN THE FOLDS OF THE BERWYN MOUNTAINS**

It was big enough news at the time to make the national press, with *The Sun* newspaper even dubbing it 'The RosWelsh Incident'. Time passed and UFOlogists advanced their theories, some believing it to be an event of such significance that it proved the existence of life in outer space. As with all such things, interest died down over the years that followed and it wasn't until 1999 that researcher Andy Roberts pieced together what might really have happened. Using official files and, crucially, an interview with Pat Evans, he concluded that a series of unrelated but simultaneous events had fuelled the legend. These included an earthquake that measured 4–5 on the Richter scale, the appearance of bolide meteors in the sky, interviewers from the British Geological Survey door-stepping

◀ A perfect camp at Llyn Lluncaws

villagers following said earthquake, and the presence of poachers up on the mountain at the alleged crash site.

While many now accept Robert's findings to provide a more likely version of events that fateful night, there are still some who swear he too has been misled. So, if you want an out-of-this-world adventure, you can't go far wrong by visiting this, the very epicentre of some proper, modern Welsh lore.

On arrival, however, you'll soon realise that a more ancient story lingers in these hills. It starts at Pistyll Rhaeadr, often cited as the UK's tallest single-drop waterfall, which in ancient Britain was thought to be the entrance to Annwn, the Celtic Otherworld. As you journey into the mountains from here, the names sing of Arthurian Legend and you will spot Arthur's Table on your OS map. There is even talk of villagers in nearby Llanrhaedr-y-Mochnant plagued by flying dragons, and a 6th-century Roman wrote of the land above this point being full of wild beasts and serpents.

You, of course, are more likely to encounter more tangible evils, such as boot-sucking bogs and mud-slick paths. But remember, after the hard work of the walk in, once you've got your tent pitched up in the stellar scenery, just keep an eye on the skies. Is it an alien or just a soaring red kite? The truth is out there.

HERE'S THE PLAN
DAY 1

1 From the car park at Tan y Pistyll turn left to walk up the road. You'll almost immediately spot – and probably hear – the waterfall from here. Keep walking, past the campsite, and you'll see a path in front of you up into the trees. Before heading off into the hills it's worth turning left here to check out the entrance to Annwn.

2 After admiring the waterfall, turn around to retrace your steps, but this time continue straight through a gate onto the track. Most people follow this wide trail to the top of the waterfall – but not you. A few steps later, you turn off the main track to follow the path down to the water. Cross the stile

TOP TIP This route can get very boggy and the path can be confusing, particularly at the head of the valley where it nears the river. Don't panic: it's only because people tend to widen the path when looking for a less boggy route. Keep heading in the same direction you were walking, with the river in view to your left, and you should soon pick it up again.

and, taking care, cross the river on the stepping stones. Once at the other side, follow the faint path diagonally uphill over the grass to join the wide gravelly track.

3 Turn left onto this track and follow it as it takes you into the valley, rising slowly and steadily above the Nant y Llyn.

4 Where the path reaches the river, the water is narrow enough to cross easily. Continue, now heading in a northwesterly direction and up to Llyn Lluncaws, your camp spot for the night. Leave the path and at the southern end of the lake you'll find a great little spot, tailor-made for a tent or bivvy.

DAY 2

5 If you can bear to wake up for sunrise, pick up the path you left and follow it round – first to the summit of Moel Sych, then northeast to the summit of Cadair Berwyn. Make sure from here that you take time to gaze down to Llandrillo and the site of the alleged UFO crash.

6 Now retrace your steps to Llyn Lluncaws to pick up your path back down to Nant y Llyn, along the valley, across the stream and back to the start.

Along the summit ridge to Cadair Berwyn (Julian Cartwright/A)

NUTS AND BOLTS

PRE-TRIP The beauty of this route is its remoteness. Even driving from the nearest village of Llanygog takes around half an hour. The best place to pick up supplies is either *en route* at Bala (if coming from the north) or Oswestry (from the east).

PUBLIC TRANSPORT Buses run to Llanygog from Oswestry (Tanat Valley Coaches; www.tanat.co.uk) as often as every hour. You will have to walk some 4km to the start of the walk from there.

WHEN TO GO If you want to follow up the UFO story, so need plenty of night-time to spot alien objects in the sky, then early or late winter are options. Be warned, though, that temperatures drop here fast, and on the hills an ice axe and crampons may be needed. For a more comfortable camp, spring or autumn are better. Summer may bring midges and tourists, but beyond the waterfall near the start the number of people you'll encounter drops dramatically.

IF YOU DON'T FANCY THE WILD CAMP? The campsite at Pistyll Rhaeadr is a good place to sleep. With its café and shorter walks from the waterfall right on your doorstep, it's a great alternative.

SHORT OF TIME? This route can be done as a day walk. Even if you don't fancy making the summit, try and get to Llyn Luncaws – a very special place.

TIME TO SPARE? Once up on the Berwyn ridge you might want to continue to Cadair Bronwen and check out Arthur's Table. Perhaps you will decide on a summit sleep on the hills, or make your way back along the ridge above the waterfall and find a spot above it to bivvy.

MORE INFO
The UFO Theory by Andy Roberts www.uk-ufo.org/condign/berwart7.htm
Pistyll Rhaeadr www.pistyllrhaeadr.co.uk/berwyns.html
Y Berwyn www.ccgc.gov.uk

Arthur's Table (Julian Cartwright/A)
Pistyll Rhaeadr (Brian Oxley/A)

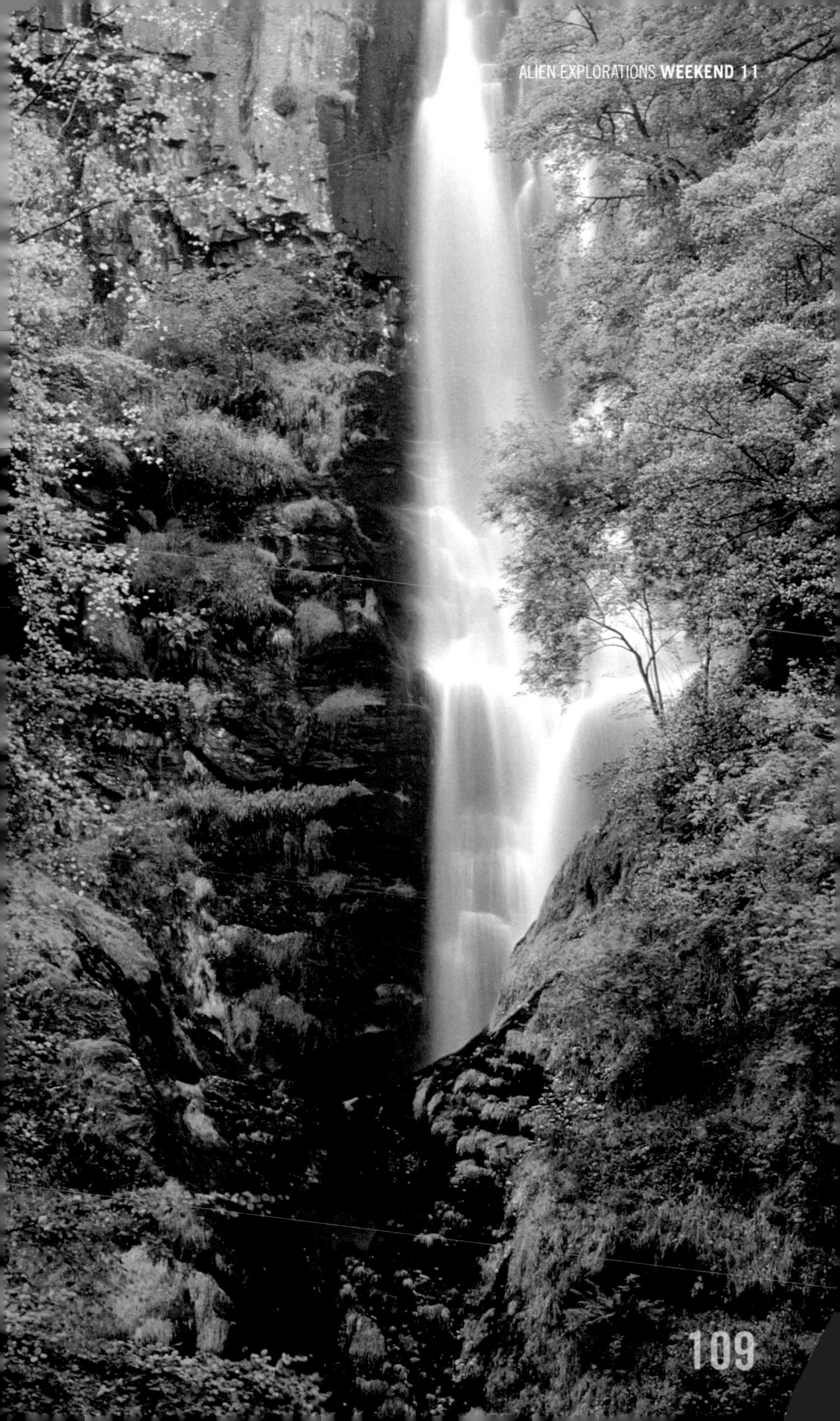

WHERE	Carneddau, Snowdonia
DURATION	1 night, 2 days
START/FINISH	Car park above Llyn Eigiau ♥ SH731662
MAPS	OS Landranger (1:50,000) 115; OS Explorer (1:25,000) 17

P eople often bemoan the lack of 'true wildness' in Wales. When they think of Snowdonia they tend to think of the Snowdon tourist trail, depositing trainloads of visitors on the summit with barely any of the required effort. But just a valley away, on the other side of Ogwen, are the Carneddau.

Formed over 400 million years ago, when volcanoes were in full flow and the land was rising from the ocean, they gained their smooth undulations courtesy of a retreating ice sheet, which left many cwms and their associated lakes pock-marking the landscape. Today, this expanse of high land boasts seven of the highest hills in Wales, and its mosaic of heather,

12 HUT AMONG THE HILLS

STAY IN AN OLD SHEPHERD'S HUT IN A REMOTE CORNER OF SNOWDONIA NATIONAL PARK, NORTH WALES

high grassland and scattered boulders is incised by winding rivers and tumbling streams.

You'd think that such a picturesque wilderness would be teeming with people – but it isn't. Or at least, not now. As long ago as the Stone Age, however, farmers were tending the land here. With the Bronze and then Iron Age came the stone hut circles, cairns and standing stones that pepper the slopes. Later, Romans erected hill forts, the Welsh and English fought for control, and eventually, after all that, people left the mountainsides.

What remains of all this history is a whole lot of wildness – and, thankfully, an old shepherd's hut, featuring two large rooms

" TODAY, THIS EXPANSE OF HIGH LAND BOASTS SEVEN OF THE HIGHEST HILLS IN WALES "

and a solid-fuel stove, maintained by the wonderful Mountain Bothies Association. The first room is the perfect place for sitting around and swapping mountain adventures. The second easily sleeps around ten to

Stone circles in Carneddau (Gail Johnson/D)

111

12 people and the ground outside is good and flat for a tent, should this be needed. Nestled at the bottom of Cwm Dulyn, it's a great spot to base yourself when exploring the traces of our human ancestors on the nearby slopes of the river and the peaks of Drum and Foel-fras.

It's not just traces of our ancestors that you'll spy when you head into this area. The Carnedds are home to a population of wild horses that have lived on this high ground for at least 500 years. Every year the local community round them up for a count to record their numbers, but the horses belong to no-one. Keep a lookout for these sturdy equines while you explore – and also for the local wildlife that includes foxes, kestrels, buzzards and, down by the river, otters.

And it's not just fauna. This area is also home to a range of hardy flora. From small Welsh poppies to much rarer Wilson's dilmy ferns, there's lots to see if you keep an eye out at ground level. Tree-wise, there's ash, hawthorn and rowan on the slopes, while most of the manmade ruins are lined with heather, mosses and lichens.

The sight of so much human history being reclaimed by nature is somehow refreshing and reassuring. When coming to wild places it's nice to know that though we do inhabit them, they are never really ours: we merely borrow them for a while – whether for hundreds of years or just a single night – and when eventually we leave, the landscape takes them back.

112

HERE'S THE PLAN
DAY 1

1 From the car park turn left onto the road and almost immediately left again, crossing the fence via the stile to reach the wide rocky track. Follow this northwest, heading towards the mound in front of you.

2 You'll reach another gate. Pass through and continue straight, ignoring the smaller paths that veer left and right, then take the main track as it ascends to your right, bearing north uphill. Soon it swings west to continue the climb, taking you away from the valley you've just been in. When you reach the other side of this hilly spur you can look down upon the wide valley below.

3 Continue on the track, passing via a series of gates and stiles. You'll see your goal well before you reach it, the stone of the building visible like a beacon. Continue on your path, which is wide and easy to follow.

4 You'll reach a fork at Melynllyn, where some begin to trek uphill to reach Foel Grach. Ignore the rough track that will take you to the lake and instead take the one that bears northwest and crosses a stream. Continue around the base of the cliffs to reach the mouth of the Dulyn Reservoir, then on to the bothy and your bed.

DAY 2

5 After the obligatory tidy of your borrowed shelter – and writing a note in the visitors' book – you can return by a different route. Walk a little

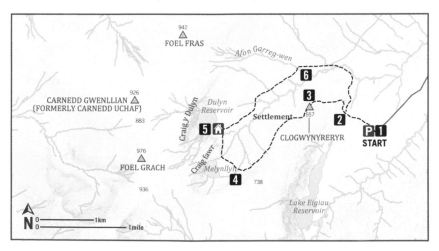

TOP TIP The ground around the Carneddau is particularly boggy so it's worth taking poles and gaiters for this weekend.

above the bothy then begin to head northeast. Almost straight away you should pick up a path that heads in the same direction, keeping you on the north side of the river. Follow it through fields, crossing the walls by stiles where needed. It can be boggy here but the path should remain clear if you keep straight.

6 The path is faint on the ground, but keep following it until, a little after Afon Garreg-wen, it forks. Take the right fork. This will take you down to the river, where you pick up a wider track at the dam and follow it to cross the Afon Dulyn. Follow it below the rocky flanks of Cerrig Cochion, heading south, until you join the first path you took at the start. Turn left and retrace your steps to the car park and your start point.

NUTS AND BOLTS

PRE-TRIP There's nowhere to grab supplies at the start of this walk. The nearest town is Llanrwst (south) or Conwy (north), so make sure you pick up what you need before heading out.

PUBLIC TRANSPORT Arriva bus line 19 runs an hourly service between Llandudno, Betws-y-Coed and Llanwrst, via Conwy and Dolgarrog, stopping at Tal-y-Bont. Unfortunately there's no way to get to the start point from there except by taxi or a very steep walk.

WHEN TO GO This is one route where a winter's frost, which freezes boggy ground, can improve the experience. Of course, it can be done year-round, though the bothy can be busy on weekends, especially bank holidays.

IF YOU DON'T FANCY THE BOTHY? If you'd rather wild camp, there's some good flat ground at Melynllyn and above the bothy overlooking Dulyn Reservoir.

SHORT OF TIME? A simple in-and-out to check out the old shepherd's hut can certainly be done in a day if you don't want to stay the night.

TIME TO SPARE? The Carneddau are a wonderfully wild and often overlooked part of Snowdonia National Park. Take the opportunity to explore not only the summits above the bothy but also the less-visited peaks of Foel-fras and Drum. You could wild camp anywhere up here or, for easy water on your doorstep, try Llyn Anafon.

MORE INFO
Up-to-date bothy conditions 👣 www.mountainbothies.org.uk
Carneddau 👣 www.nationaltrust.org.uk/carneddau-and-glyderau
Snowdonia 👣 www.eryri-npa.gov.uk
Local 👣 www.llanrwst.net

A Carneddau ponies (The Photolibrary Wales/A)

13 ROCKY ROMAN STEPS

SCRAMBLE ALONG AN ANCIENT ROMAN TRAIL
INTO THE HIDDEN HEART OF THE RHINOGS, MID WALES

WHERE	Rhinogs, Mid Wales
DURATION	1 night, 2 days
START/FINISH	Cwm Bychan campsite and car park ♀ SH645315
MAPS	OS Landranger (1:50,000) 124; OS Explorer (1:25,000) 18

I f there's anywhere in the rest of the UK that can rival Scotland for sheer wilderness it has to be the Rhinogs. Little known outside hill-walking and mountaineering circles, this fairly compact range of peaks offers a true taste of solitude.

Small though the Rhinogs may appear on the OS map, they offer a much tougher prospect on the ground, and the journey in kilometres doesn't convey the arduous reality of crossing these relatively short distances. Photographs show fairly innocuous – though stunningly picturesque – peaks, but hiding among the heather are giant rocky crevices, left behind courtesy of the last ice age. Indeed, it's probably the difficulty of crossing this range – along with the fact that its more famous Snowdonian cousins are much easier to access – that has kept it off most people's 'must visit' list.

The only time the Rhinogs ever came close to the headlines was in 1846, when gold was discovered here. Today there may be no gold, but there's still hidden treasure, in the form of a superb wilderness experience.

> " **THERE'S STILL HIDDEN TREASURE, IN THE FORM OF A SUPERB WILDERNESS EXPERIENCE** "

The easiest way to unlock this seemingly impenetrable area of mountains is via the so-called Roman Steps that lead up from the Llyn Cwm Bychan side of the massif. 'Steps', however, is something of a misnomer. The path is actually just a very well-preserved medieval packhorse trail and drovers' road that was once the main route between Chester (a Roman stronghold) and the fortified bastion of Harlech Castle. So don't arrive expecting a die-straight route taking you effortlessly from your car into the remote hinterland. Instead, this fairly narrow trail cuts between two walls of rock, where even the sunlight struggles to penetrate. It undulates through the vegetation as the flanks of the mountains rise and finally deposits you near a faint path that, if you can find it, will take you into the heart of the range near to the base of Rhinog Fawr – one of the peaks that gives the area its name.

Picking up the path to Llyn Du will take much longer than you expect, but the effort is well worth it, for here, in the shadow of one of the wildest mountains in the national park, you can spend the night.

The Rhinogs, as well as forming part of a National Nature Reserve, are also declared a Biogenetic Reserve, which is one of several habitats protected for the benefit of European wildlife. Birdlife can be especially rewarding here. Keep an eye out for ring ouzels, rare relatives of the blackbird, which return from Africa every March to nest in the rocky crevices above you. Other species include northern wheatears, which nest in grassy holes, black and red grouse, and birds of prey, including kestrels, peregrine falcons and the occasional hen harrier quartering the heather. This area has all the potential for extending your adventure into a longer, wilder exploration. Or you could just take a weekend to relax by the water and watch the wild world go by.

HERE'S THE PLAN
DAY 1

1 Don't leave the car park via the way you drove in. Instead, head west, uphill to the gate to the farm. Pass through and turn right to pick up a clear path south. You'll start to gain height almost straight away, moving first over farmland then through woods and finally onto more open hillside.

2 The going is fairly easy at this point as the path winds over streams and around rocky outcrops. You'll come to a wall and a gate. Pass through and turn left to begin your ascent of the Roman Steps.

3 This stretch is one of the highlights of the walk and feels as though you're traversing a rocky

Male black grouse square up (Erni/S) ➤
Hiking the Rhinogs is wild, rocky and remote ➤

passageway surrounded by mountains. It may take longer than you think but you will, at last, reach a large pile of stones. Pass to the left of this and begin descending. You'll get some great views here of Llyn Trawsfynydd and a forestry area.

4 Soon a sign will warn that you're in wild country and should take care. A little after this, a broken wall appears on your right. Leave the main path here and begin to cut south. It's downhill to the start of the path, over mainly long grass and wet terrain. From this point the going becomes rocky: you'll need to use your hands in a couple of places, and it may seem to take an inordinately long time to cover what appears a relatively short distance on the map. But persevere: just when you think it continues for ever, like magic, you'll emerge on the shores of Llyn Du and your resting place for the night.

DAY 2

5 The hardy and experienced might want to try a summit of Rhinog Fawr or may be tempted to return via the very pretty lake of Gloyw Lyn. Both are options but, be warned, both are challenging, requiring some scrambling and excellent navigational skills. There are many boulders to negotiate, plus slabs with big drops between them – almost like crevasses. Be sure you know what you are taking on. Otherwise, simply retrace your steps from yesterday to reach the car once more.

TOP TIP Don't expect to cover distance quickly in the Rhinogs: the going is always tough. To avoid nasty surprises, plan to take your time and enjoy it. In bad weather, navigation is particularly difficult, so don't be afraid to change your plans if conditions change.

NUTS AND BOLTS

PRE-TRIP There are no supplies at the farm so be sure to grab something at either Harlech (north) or Barmouth (south), the nearest towns, before you arrive. Take small change with you to pay for parking at the farm. If you get there too late to head out immediately, then a night in the campsite at the start is not only cheap but also a fantastic option. Pitch near to Llyn Cwm Bychan for a perfect sunset surrounded by these truly wild peaks and wake refreshed ready to tackle the Rhinogs in the morning.

PUBLIC TRANSPORT There is currently no public transport to the Rhinogs. The nearest you can get is Harlech, which has a train station. It's around 10km from there to the start of this walk. A taxi is an option.

WHEN TO GO Spring and summer offer the best chance of good weather. This is not somewhere you want to tackle if the weather is playing up.

IF YOU DON'T FANCY THE WILD CAMP? As mentioned above, staying at the campsite is an excellent alternative. It has no website and you can't book; it's a turn-up-and-pitch affair with an honesty box. Delightful!

SHORT OF TIME? The hike up to Llyn Du and back makes for a good day walk, and even just a stay in the campsite at the farm will offer a tantalising flavour of this uncrowded part of Snowdonia.

TIME TO SPARE? If you know what you're doing, the Rhinogs offer ample exploring opportunities. Whether you want to tick off a summit, check out one of the other two lakes nearby, complete a large loop around the peaks or just linger in the mountains, the choice is yours.

MORE INFO

Local ✇ www.harlech.com; www.barmouth-wales.co.uk
Rhinogydd ✇ www.ccgc.gov.uk
Snowdonia ✇ www.visitsnowdonia.info

Llyn Du, beneath Rhinog Fawr

WHERE	Grwyne Fawr, South Wales
DURATION	1 night, 2 days
START/FINISH	Blaen-y-cwm car park ♥ SO253284
MAPS	OS Landranger (1:50,000) 161; OS Explorer (1:25,000) 13

Being the Black Mountains can't be easy. In fact, it must be like being the youngest in a family of four siblings. Making up just one quarter of the ranges that define the Brecon Beacons National Park, it constantly has to fight to be noticed. And it certainly has a fight on its hands: the Brecon Beacons, in the centre, are way more popular and boast some of Britain's biggest peaks south of Birmingham; Fforest Fawr – also known as 'The great forest' – gets all the mountain bikers' attention for its stunning network of tyre-friendly trails; and the Black Mountain in the west virtually shares its name, meaning that people are forever confusing the two. Yes, it seems

14 THE FORGOTTEN SIBLING

**HIKE HIGH INTO THE BLACK MOUNTAINS
IN THE LITTLE-KNOWN EASTERN END
OF BRECON BEACONS NATIONAL PARK, SOUTH WALES**

that this range – which spreads east of the park as far as the border with Herefordshire in England – is forever cast in the shadow of the rest. But that's good news for wilderness lovers. Thanks to the crowd-pulling appeal of the other three, it's actually the perfect place in which to your spend your own secluded night watching the stars.

Separated physically from its siblings by the River Wye, there is no denying that the Black Mountains landscape looks a little different. There are fewer crashing waterfalls and steep escarpments. Instead you'll find high, rolling sandstone, studded with lumps of limestone and incised with silty riverbeds. There are also fewer of the dramatic glacial cwms and drops than among the peaks of North Wales. The valley may have been formed by an ice sheet – though some geologists go so far as to say that it may have

> " HERE IN THE BLACK MOUNTAINS, YOU CAN KEEP YOUR FEET FIRMLY ON THE GROUND AND STILL FEEL ON TOP OF THE WORLD "

Gospel Pass, the Black Mountains (Davidmartyn/D)

completely escaped the big freeze during the last ice age. Either way, the geology makes for some extraordinary colours, which change dramatically with the seasons: from auburn dunes of thick sediment, to maroon and even greyish-purple.

The best thing about this area – aside from the lack of crowds – is its topography, which means that once you get up high, you stay high. Thus planning a high-level meander is easy, as is pitching your tent on one of the many flattened summits. It also scores points on natural history grounds: its slopes support unusual plants such as whitebeams, liverworts and various lichens, plus such breeding upland birds as red grouse and golden plover.

And it's not only birds that take to the air up here: this area is also very popular with gliders. So as you make your way along the tops that line the Grwyne Valley, listen out for the unmistakeable whoosh from those manmade wings. And later, as you watch the day turn to dusk, fire up your camping stove and watch the lights begin to twinkle in the villages at your feet, you'll revel in a secret that the gliders don't know: that here in the Black Mountains, you can keep your feet firmly on the ground and still feel on top of the world.

Golden plovers breed on the Black Mountains (Dalia Kvedaraite/D)
Looking to Pen y Gadair Fawr from Waun Fach.

HERE'S THE PLAN
DAY 1

1 From the car park follow the path which will lead you temporarily out onto the road. Turn right and follow it for a few steps then take the path on your right leading uphill. Soon afterwards, take the less-defined path that heads up sharply in a northerly direction and follow it for about 1km up onto the ridge above the valley.

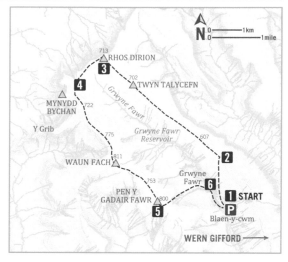

2 Here you'll join a much more defined track that runs northwest to southeast. Turn left onto it and follow it northwest. Already the views are spectacular and though it can be boggy up here the going is straightforward, so continue all the way to Twyn Talycefn and beyond,

TOP TIP There is nowhere easy to collect water on this route without climbing a long way down and then back up again, so take plenty with you. If you get stuck after Rhos Dirion you can easily descend to Grwyne Fawr to collect some – though it will be a pain!

staying true to the northwest line. You will, at last, reach the top of Rhos Dirion. It's a fairly flat summit but, its position right on the edge of this huge plateau allows commanding views into the towns and villages beyond – and also of the route you'll take tomorrow. On a windy day you might want to consider moving on to the next stage and finding one of the hollows around Mynydd Bychan that offer a little more shelter. Otherwise pitch your tent/bivvy, get the stove on and enjoy the views.

DAY 2

3 Leave the summit by the obvious path southwest towards the col and fence line. Much like yesterday's path, the high ground can be very wet so it can take a little longer as you look for detours. Continue, taking the gate through the fence. Be sure not to pick up the path that sweeps you out to Y Grib: instead take the left-hand path at the fork, bearing southeast.

4 This next part is probably the worst for bogs and peat hags, so perhaps grab a snack before you knuckle down to it. Then follow the path, tracking roughly southeast to the summit of Waun Fach. The path undulates, with many diversions around standing water, but once at Waun Fach the end is in sight. Continue along this boggy plateau, first descending then reascending, until you reach the summit of Pen y Gadair Fawr.

5 The views from here make the effort well worth it. Linger a while to enjoy your reward then, when you're ready, turn your back on the summit and look northeast. You should see a rough path leading off in the same direction. It's not on the map, but is fairly well defined and cuts downhill alongside (but not in) the forestry land, making the descent quick, if fairly steep. Follow this all the way down. You'll pass the remains of old homesteads just before reaching the stream, where handy boulders enable you to cross easily into the woods.

6 From here turn right onto the path and follow it along under cover of the trees, keeping the stream to your left. Soon you'll come to a bridge. Turn left to cross it and then make your way up to the minor road. Turn right onto it and shortly you'll reach the car park and your start point.

TOP Heading to Rhos Dirion
CENTRE The stream at step 5; The camp at the summit
BOTTOM The view from Mynydd Bychan

NUTS AND BOLTS

PRE-TRIP There is nothing in the way of shops at the start, so you will need to collect supplies before you arrive. Abergavenny is the nearest town; other options are Crickhowell, Hay-on-Wye (north) or Hereford (northwest). Any one of these is also an option for an overnight if you fancy a B&B or hotel pre-trip.

PUBLIC TRANSPORT This is another wild weekend that lies beyond public transport. The nearest you can get to the start is Wern Gifford (via bus from Abergavenny or Hereford). But it's still a 15km walk from there so you may consider a taxi or else have to bring your car.

WHEN TO GO As with other boggy routes, winter frost can actually improve things – though don't forget that this time of year often means more rain. But this really is a camp that can be enjoyed all year and, being less visited than the nearby big-hitters of Pen y Fan et al, you're unlikely to meet crowds or have any problems with finding space.

IF YOU DON'T FANCY THE SUMMIT CAMP? The land up here is truly wild and spacious so there are lots of options below the summit for placing your tent. More secluded spots lurk on the edges near Y Das and Mynydd Bychan.

SHORT OF TIME? Once you've camped you could retrace your steps or simply cut down into the valley and Grwyne Fawr and return on the path alongside the reservoir. This makes for a much quicker descent.

TIME TO SPARE? It would be tempting to take your time and explore more of these hills. From the summit of Rhos Dirion you could turn northeast and check out the famous Lord Hereford's Knob (Twmpa) and kip up there. Or continue along the ridge from the summit of Pen y Gadair Fawr. You'll see in the summer that many people camp alongside the river in the woods (fairly near the car park), which is also an option.

MORE INFO

Black Mountains ☷ www.breconbeacons.org/black-mountains
Local ☷ www.visitcrickhowell.co.uk; www.visitabergavenny.co.uk
Mid Wales ☷ www.visitmidwales.co.uk

Hiking the track up to Lord Hereford's Knob (Cody Duncan/A)

> " WHEN YOU WAKE UP TO THAT EXQUISITE VISTA IN THE MORNING, AS SUNRISE TINGES THE DARK HILLS WITH AN ORANGE BLUSH, REMIND YOURSELF THAT IT HAS COST YOU NOTHING TO SPEND THE NIGHT ON THIS MOUNTAIN MATTRESS "

SCOTLAND

WHERE	Dumfries and Galloway
DURATION	1 night, 2 days
START/FINISH	Glen Trool car park ♀ NX414802
MAPS	OS Landranger (1:50,000) 77; OS Explorer (1:25,000) 318

I t's easy to get blindsided by the majesty of the Scottish Highlands, where things can feel properly wild. However, there is another exciting Scottish wilderness that many of us miss as we speed north along the A74, and that is the Southern Uplands. Lying west of the main road, this region has its fair share of blinding peaks. What's more, the Galloway National Park – within which this route sits – was the first in the UK to be designated a Dark Sky Reserve, meaning that its distance from light pollution makes it the perfect place to go stargazing.

This wild weekend not only offers stars in the sky but also several at ground level – of the hilly variety. You may have heard of The Merrick, a rounded

15 THE AWFUL HAND

SCALE A LITTLE-KNOWN LANDSCAPE OF STRANGE PEAKS AND EVEN STRANGER NAMES IN SCOTLAND'S SOUTHERN UPLANDS, GALLOWAY NATIONAL PARK

lump of a peak and the highest in the area, ticked off by many walkers as they head out from the Glen Trool car park. However, four others are also well worth looking out for, if only for the name. Along with The Merrick, Benyellary, Kirriereoch Hill, Tarfessock and Shalloch on Minnoch make up The Awful Hand, a chain of peaks that on your OS map appear

> **THIS WILD WEEKEND OFFERS NOT ONLY STARS IN THE SKY BUT ALSO SEVERAL AT GROUND LEVEL**

– with a healthy dose of imagination – to make up the rough shape of a giant hand, with Benyellary as the thumb and the Shalloch of Minnoch as the little finger. Hence the name.

But it's not just the peaks that hold intriguing monikers. Explore further and you'll find The Dungeon Hills – the range to the east of the hand; The Grey Man of Merrick – a rocky protrusion that resembles a man's face (more convincingly than the hills resemble an actual hand); and The Murder Hole – a place featured in *The Raiders*, by Samuel Crockett.

Sunset view to The Ayrshire coast from The Merrick (Rod McLean/A)

133

Crockett's book is certainly worth a read before visiting. It tells the tale of problems between smugglers on the Solway Coast and the gypsies of Galloway, and is rammed full of wild landscape and bloody murder, with a dash of local history and a soupçon of folk legend. And even as you begin this adventure you'll be reminded of some real-life gory history. At the car park stands the massive granite slab of Bruce's Stone. This marks the site of the Battle of Glen Trool when, in 1307, Robert the Bruce won his first victory over the English Army in the Scottish Wars of Independence.

From there you can begin the climb up to The Merrick, passing through felled forestry, past a former bothy and over some fairly boggy ground until you reach the top. From the summits you'll get a real feel for these oft-forgotten hills and even spy the Solway Coast and Cumbria's Lake District beyond.

Once you've completed as much or as little of the walk as you'd like, you can begin your descent to Loch Enoch. According to Crockett, sand was once collected here for sharpening scythes and knives. Now a beauty spot only, it's ideal for a wild camp. Be sure you pass through the gate and continue until you begin to see little spits of sand at the water's edge. Though not the softest place to lay your head, they are certainly less saturated than the long grass. Choose the perfect one and you could enjoy views of the sun setting behind The Merrick before the stars come out to play.

As the sky darkens and the moon casts shadows on the loch, you can see why this wild spot became the inspiration for stories. Now, after your night in the wild, you'll have one of your own to tell.

HERE'S THE PLAN
DAY 1

1 Leaving the car park at Bruce's Stone, take the marked track to The Merrick. It's a slow and steady start as the track begins to weave uphill. The views will begin to open out before you. Keep climbing, first on open ground then through the forest, until you come to the old bothy at Culsharg.

2 This bothy was once used regularly by walkers and even maintained by the MBA, but no longer. A stay is possible if you're desperate, but nowadays it seems more visitors use it as an outhouse than a bedroom! Continue past this and alongside the forestry land. You'll start to head uphill once more, the ground becoming boggier as a network of streams slice through the marshy terrain beneath your feet.

3 Begin your climb to the summit of the first peak of The Awful Hand: Benyellary. Continue on the path, heading northwest, over the ridge of Neive of the Spit, for the final steep pull up to the highest peak: The Merrick.

4 From the top of the Southern Uplands' highest peak you should be able to see Ailsa Craig. This volcanic plug has a history that encompasses pirates, Spanish invasion, smuggling and quarrying for its rare rock used to make curling stones, but is now home only to hundreds of breeding puffins and gannets. You'll also see the other peaks that form the digits of The Awful Hand: to the southwest, the so-called thumb of Benyellary; ahead of you, in order, Kirriereoch Hill, Tarfessock and Shalloch on Minnoch. Those feeling energetic may decide to tackle the whole lot. If so, be warned: Shalloch is a fair old yomp away, with barely a recognisable summit, while Kirriereoch and Tarfessock are easy to link together but require lots of descent and reascent (this hand is called 'awful' for a reason). If you're

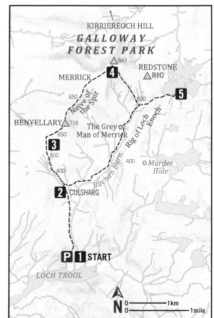

TOP TIP Galloway Forest is one of only a couple of officially designated Dark Sky Reserves in the UK, meaning its lack of light pollution allows for a clear view of the night sky (providing it's not cloudy). So why not take along a guide to some constellations you might see? The easiest to identify is The Plough. From here you can locate the North Star/Polaris. You may be lucky enough to see Jupiter, the Milky Way and – on a clear night – even the Northern Lights.

feeling up to it, then the best way is to waste no time and head there and back from here. There are few paths, but the tracks of previous hill-walkers will be obvious.

From The Merrick's summit you'll already have spied Loch Enoch from the top. Make a beeline for it on a faint track, bearing southeast down the flanks of Redstone Rig. There is no path marked on the OS map but you will spy one made by other walkers. Watch for the rocky outcrops and look before you step, as sudden drops of a couple of metres or more are common. You'll eventually arrive at a fence line. Cross this on a stile near the loch end then follow it down to the loch.

The route now traces the water's edge, where the saturated ground is often quite boggy. The long grass here makes a reasonable camping option but you will find better sites where you emerge onto the first of several sand spits on the loch shore. With views of The Merrick on one side, The Dungeons on the other and an expanse of loch to reflect the sunset, this is a perfect pitch.

DAY 2

5 Start the morning by retracing your steps back to the fence. Cross it, then follow it southwest on a narrow but fairly obvious path. At around grid ref ♀ NX435844 you'll spy some rocky outcrops, where you will meet The Grey Man of Merrick. After taking the obligatory shot of his incredibly detailed face, continue on the path as it follows Buchan Burn. The going through the forest can be rough and overgrown, so take walking poles to help fight your way through.

You'll eventually emerge onto a forestry track that leads to Culsharg bothy. From there, retrace your steps to the start.

A line of Scots pines by the side of Loch Trool, Galloway Forest Park (Creative Nature Media/S)

NUTS AND BOLTS

PRE-TRIP Pick up any food you may need in Newton Stewart before you go. Cunningham's usually carries camping gas and meals. A visitor centre at Glentrool has maps, tea and cake.

PUBLIC TRANSPORT The nearest train station to Glentrool is Barrhill, National Express also run coaches to Newton Stewart. Local bus company Kings of Kircowan runs the daily service 359 between Newton Stewart and Girvan, stopping at Glentrool village; from Barrhill (for train connections) or Newton Stewart it will take around 25 minutes. Call ☎ 01671 830284 for timetable information. Buses can be infrequent, especially in winter, so check beforehand.

WHEN TO GO This place is good all year. However, you'll find it quieter, and be more likely to have Loch Enoch to yourself – without people and with fewer midges – if you go in spring or autumn (avoiding half term/Easter holiday weeks).

IF YOU DON'T FANCY THE LOCH? There are certainly other camp spots in the area. You might try a summit sleep if you're prepared to carry in or hike for your water, or you could try one of several local bothies – either sleeping in them or camping outside. Check the MBA website, or look for buildings on the map: there are also many bothies that are not maintained by the organisation.

SHORT OF TIME? If you're just longing for the camp then you could miss out The Merrick summit entirely and just head straight to Loch Enoch and out the same way – passing the Grey Man, via the same route.

TIME TO SPARE? If you have two cars or are happy to fork out for a taxi (costs about £40), you could leave your car at Bruce's Stone and then get a taxi to the car park by Loch Riecawr. From here it's about an hour's walk-in to an MBA bothy, where you can stay the first night. This puts you in a prime place to tackle the whole Awful Hand without requiring a dog-leg journey. Starting with a thigh-busting climb up to Shalloch, it still involves a lot of ups and downs, but then you end on The Merrick, with the option to tackle the thumb of Benyellary, before heading down for your second night at the perfect camp spot by Loch Enoch. Leave by following the same route as described back out to your car/other car at Bruce's Stone car park.

MORE INFO

Galloway Forest Park 🖥 www.gallowayforestpark.com
Forestry Commission for Galloway 🖥 http://scotland.forestry.gov.uk/forest-parks/
    galloway-forest-park
Visit Scotland 🖥 www.visitscotland.com
Mountain Bothies Association 🖥 www.mountainbothies.org.uk
Background 📖 *The Raiders* by Samuel Crockett, Canongate Classics

Come face to face with the Grey Man of Merrick. ➤

16 A PINT TOO FAR?

WALK TO THE UK'S MOST REMOTE PUB, ON THE KNOYDART PENINSULA, SCOTTISH HIGHLANDS

WHERE	Lochaber, Scottish Highlands
DURATION	2 days, 1 night
START	Barrisdale Bay ♀ NG873059
FINISH	Inverie Harbour ♀ NG764001
MAPS	OS Landranger (1:50,000) 33; OS Explorer (1:25,000) 413

How far would you walk for a pint? It's a question a walker, especially one heading to the wilder places of the UK, will often ask themselves. That first sip of a post-walk ale – the moment when you know you have done what you set out to do, followed the plan and all has ended well – is the sensation that sees you heading out to wild places again and again. So it's fitting, perhaps, that this walk's main aim centres on reaching a pub. But it isn't just any old hostelry: this is officially the remotest pub in mainland Britain. Those wanting to sup on the sweet amber nectar and local ales inside can get there by one of only two ways: by boat or on foot.

That's because this place isn't called a wilderness for nothing. Located between the two lochs of Nevis and Hourn (also known as the 'lochs of heaven and hell' – mainly by those who've walked the land that sits between) is the Knoydart Peninsula, a tight mountainous cluster of contour lines that stretches out into the sea. Sure, it has a road. Just the one: an 11km of tarmac that sits alone, not connected to the rest of the UK road network. And it's at the end of that road that the fun really starts.

Home to four Munros (Scottish mountains over 3,000ft), this region is something of a Graceland for hill-walkers. Its crystal-clear lochs, scattered between the great toothy jawline of peaks and often veiled beneath a tantalising layer of cloud, is a slice of wild paradise. Here hikers will often find themselves outnumbered by red deer and perhaps even scrutinised by a soaring golden eagle. Some call it the 'last great wilderness'. In the right weather, meandering along the path from the pebble-crusted beach at Barisdale, passing the rustic farmhouses further up and descending from the col between Stob a' Chearcaill and Luinne Bheinn, it can feel perfectly walker-friendly.

> **"**
> **HERE HIKERS WILL OFTEN FIND THEMSELVES OUTNUMBERED BY RED DEER**
> **"**

Catch it on a bad day, though, and it can feel harsh and lonely, suitable only for the wildlife. Either way, whether you start at the beauty of Barrisdale Bay, the car-friendly Loch Hourn, or even just cheat and take the ferry direct to Inverie, this place is bound to leave a profound impression.

◄ A perfect tent spot above Loch an Dubh-Lochain

Every paradise comes with a history and Knoydart is no exception. Its tumultuous past, with battles between rich landowners and hardworking locals, could inspire a Hollywood epic. It's hard to imagine today, but in 1852 Knoydart was home to around 400 crofters, who fished in the waters and grew crops on the land. However, in typical Clearances fashion, the landowners wanted more profit from their acreage – either in sheep farming (the value of wool was high) or in deer hunting for rich aristocrats from London. Landlord Josephine MacDonnell told the villagers to evacuate; their back rent owing would be forgotten and they could start a new life in Canada. It's estimated that over 330 left but, depending on whose account you read – remembering, of course, that history from that time has been muddied by skewed records and contradictory accounts – 60 people (comprising 11 families) refused to go. A messy dispute ensued, with many being forcibly removed and their belongings thrown into the loch.

After World War II, history seemed to repeat itself. Knoydart had famously been used as a training ground for British troops – much to the disdain of landowners and Nazi sympathisers Lord and Lady Brocket. They returned to their estate, disposing of everything the 'scum' military may have used, and promptly sacked all the local workers. Fresh from a bitter war, and in desperate need of land in order to carve a new living for themselves, this was a step too far for locals. In 1948, the Knoydart Seven (as they are now known) raided the Brockets' estate in an attempt to reclaim a

142

tiny portion of the land for themselves – just 10,000 of a possible 200,000 acres. The law seemed to be on their side, with new post-war legislation that allowed local people to utilise land for their livelihood. MPs in London backed them and they secured the services of a lawyer. Unfortunately it all went wrong when said lawyer advised them to play by the book and leave the land they had seized – thus forfeiting their squatters' rights, which was their one bargaining chip. The Brockets jumped on this opportunity, the MPs quickly got cold feet and when it went to the Secretary of State for a hearing, the case was lost.

The Knoydart Seven may have lost the battle, but their actions resonated over the years to come. It set a precedent for future disputes between working class and aristocracy, giving other communities the courage to challenge absentee landowners who preserved swathes of countryside for use by playboys rather than locals. It's heartening to know also that since 1999, 71km^2 now make up the Knoydart estate, which is owned by a foundation of locals and not-for-profit groups who work hard to protect the land from development and privatisation.

Given that we walkers are now free not only to walk around the peninsula but also to explore off the paths and wild camp, those brave protestors did in one sense win their battle. So when you visit Inverie, take a minute to thank them by showing your respect at the simple memorial that was laid to them outside the Post Office in 1981. As you walk in from Barrisdale Bay, however, before you descend through the woodland above Inverie down to the hamlet and campsite at Long Beach, you'll notice a cross on a hillock to the right of your path. Many mistake this as the memorial to the Knoydart Seven but, ironically, it was actually placed here by Lord Brocket for his family.

The place is now, of course, very peaceful. Just some 100 people live here – often fewer in winter – though in summer this number can more than triple with day-trippers and overnighters. In the village itself you'll find the aforementioned post office, a primary school, several options for accommodation and, of course, the *Guinness Book of Records* record-holding pub: the Old Forge. Enjoy your remotest pint in Britain – you've earned it! – then retire to what is, quite frankly, one of the best and most beautiful campsites in the world, down the road at Long Beach. With the isles of Skye, Rum and Eigg all visible from your tent flaps, it's the one instance you'll find in this book where paying for the campsite (a steal at £4) seems a preferable choice to camping wild.

HERE'S THE PLAN
DAY 1

1 Take the ferry from Mallaig to Barrisdale Bay (pre-booking essential; see page 148). Depending on the tide, you'll probably land near some rocks, over which you'll need to scramble to reach the beach. Once at the beach, after stopping to admire the views of this jaw-droppingly beautiful slice of wild sand, head inland where you pick up the path heading southwest.

2 Shortly you'll pass a sign telling you that Barisdale is just ten minutes walk away. There you'll find a campsite and a bunkhouse/bothy (charge), which offers a stopover for those wanting to linger. Those needing to press on, however, should follow the path past the tents and buildings towards a copse with a white building. As you get closer, take the path where it turns to your right and, ignoring the fork on your left, cross the stream via a bridge and continue as it climbs steadily uphill.

3 Soon the vista really opens up, offering incredible views over the surrounding mountains and back to Barrisdale Bay. Continue climbing, crossing a stream and traversing under some trees. You're now heading into the heart of the terrain and will soon spy the col of two mountains coming up ahead. The cairn at the top is a fantastic place to stop for a bite.

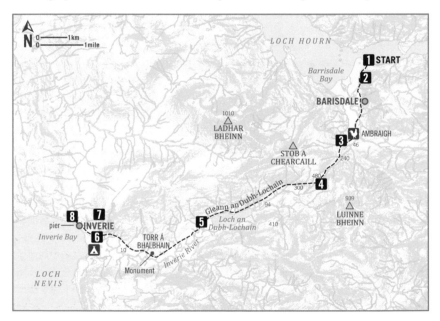

If you're to meet any other walkers on this route then it will be here. From this point, Munro-baggers (those on a mission to scale all the mountains in Scotland over 3,000ft) begin their climb of Ladhar Bheinn.

4 If planning to break the trip into an extra day/night then you'll find a good spot to camp or bivvy at the loch edge towards which you'll be walking from here. Continue on the path – which gets really boggy (especially after heavy rain) – and skirt the loch.

5 Soon you'll spy the tiny hill with the cross adorning its summit – erected by Lord Brocket to honour his family. Continue heading towards it on the well-defined path until you are virtually underneath. You can easily scramble up for a closer look. Otherwise follow the path, which now climbs uphill slightly into some trees. Continue on and through the wooden gate.

6 Take the lower path as it winds down alongside the wall and soon joins the tarmac road at the bottom. For one of the best campsites in the UK turn left, passing houses and a camping barn/hostel, and emerge on the seashore. Here, for just £4, you can pitch your tent, with the rare luxury of a compost toilet, fresh water on tap and money-can't-buy views over to

TOP Barrisdale Bay
BOTTOM The pretty hamlet of Inverie; A loo with a view at Long Beach campsite

TOP TIP To avoid going hungry after your big walk to the pub it is essential that you pre-book your meal. You can do this online (🖱 www.theoldforge.co.uk) but it's best to call and confirm too, as there will be no other options by the time you arrive.

Rum and Skye. If you're dying for your pint – or your pre-booked mealtime is fast approaching – then turn right and the road will take you all the way to the pub for your well-deserved reward.

DAY 2

7 Take the morning to explore the tiny settlement at Inverie, making time to discover the museum and learn about the history of the hardy souls, past and present, who have lived on this wild and isolated peninsula. There's a great coffee shop on the main street and a post office if you fancy sending a postcard.

8 Continue along the road and soon you'll reach the turning on your left for the harbour. From here you can take the ferry back to Mallaig.

A well-earned drink awaits at The Old Forge ⚑

TOP Peering into Knoydart from the water
CENTRE The facilities at Long Beach; View from the tent at Long Beach
BOTTOM The Old Forge

NUTS AND BOLTS

PRE-TRIP You will need to book your place on the ferries in advance – both to Barisdale and Mallaig (from Inverie). The former does not offer this service on a daily basis; the latter offers a choice of departure times – more in summer than in winter – so you can decide whether or not you want extra time to explore the peninsula.

PUBLIC TRANSPORT Trains run regularly from Fort William to Mallaig. A good option for those in the south or north of England is to take the sleeper train from London, Crewe or Preston to Fort William, arriving early morning, then catch the onward train to Mallaig. The journey takes around 12 hours. Buses also go to Mallaig from Fort William (🖱 www.shielbuses.co.uk). If you're coming from Skye, you can take the Caledonian MacBrayne ferry from Armadale (🖱 www.calmac.co.uk).

WHEN TO GO Knoydart is a magical place all year. To avoid midges and crowds, May or September are good options. Snow may remain on the high Munros into spring and even early summer, so if you plan to take in any of the hills make sure you are prepared. Ferry services are less frequent in the winter so call ahead. Summer can be busy in Inverie and Mallaig.

IF YOU DON'T FANCY THE CAMPSITE? There are a couple of great wild camp spots in the valley on the way down to Loch an Dubh-Lochain. If the weather is good you can camp high near the pass between the Munros – though you'll need to carry in enough water for the night unless you fancy a round trip of 6km to the loch and back. Another spot is along the edge of the loch itself. Note, though, that there are fragile eco-systems on Knoydart and lots of local wildlife so if signs advise against camping obey them and do not light fires at any time. In Inverie there is the option of the bunkhouse, hostel and a variety of B&B and self-catering accommodation (🖱 www.visitknoydart.co.uk).

SHORT OF TIME? If you're a very fast walker then you could try to walk fast from Barisdale, catch your pint then grab the last ferry over to Mallaig. But you'd definitely lose part of the experience doing that, not to mention one of the best sunsets in the UK.

TIME TO SPARE? It would cost extra to be dropped off but some people like to walk the whole peninsula, starting at Loch Hourn (adds 6km of rough coastal track). A boat definitely offers the easiest access to this, though, as the land route is an arduous, winding, single-track road that – though only 19km – takes much longer than it sounds. Local taxis might take you there (fairly pricey, as they will expect you to pay for their return journey), but otherwise you will have to drive and walk in and out to Inverie the same way, which can be a bit dull and feel like less of a proper journey. There is, however, a farm at the start of the track that offers a B&B option plus tea, coffee and snacks (🖱 www.kinlochhourn.com). If walking in from Loch Hourn, or coming in from Barrisdale Bay but wanting to take your time, you could camp at Barisdale bothy/bunkhouse, and spend the day ambling around this picturesque and wild beach before moving on to Inverie. Those with even more time, plus serious energy and map-reading skills, might want to add a couple of Munros to their itinerary. Note, however, that these are on very rough ground and often pathless.

MORE INFO
Local 🖱 www.knoydart-foundation.com
The Old Forge 🖱 www.theoldforge.co.uk
Ferries 🖱 www.knoydartferry.com and westernislescruises.co.uk

WHERE	Mallaig, Scotland
DURATION	1 night, 2 days
START/FINISH	Mallaig Harbour ♀ NM677971
MAPS	OS Landranger (1:50,000) 40; OS Explorer (1:25,000) 398

Everyone knows about Nessie. Hordes of tourists every year pay for a boat trip on Scotland's most famous loch hoping to catch a glimpse of the legendary lost plesiosaur – or whatever they think the fabled Loch Ness Monster might be. But who wants to rub shoulders with a coachload of people when you can journey to an altogether quieter patch of water and look for your own monster from the porch of your tent?

Morag – the alleged resident of the freshwater Loch Morar (which, at a whopping 310m is also the deepest water body of its kind in the British Isles) – was first seen as far back as 1887. Numerous sightings have since

17 LOCH LESS-KNOWN MONSTER

CAMP ON THE WILD SHORES OF LOCH MORAR, HOME TO SCOTLAND'S 'OTHER' FABLED MONSTER OF THE LOCHS, IN MALLAIG, WESTERN ISLES

been reported, most recently in 2013 when a couple on holiday swore they saw a large serpent-like creature in the waves. Reports vary but what they do seem to agree on is that Morag is brown, has three humps and is around 30ft (9m) in length. In 1969, a couple of brothers claimed to have had a close encounter when they struck her with their speedboat (and Morag, apparently, retaliated). In 1970, the Loch Ness Investigation Bureau expanded its search area to include Loch Morar. Not that you'd know that now. There's no pomp or fanfare around this body of water, no museum or cuddly toy: just one of the best two-day adventures you can have.

> **NUMEROUS SIGHTINGS HAVE SINCE BEEN REPORTED, MOST RECENTLY IN 2013**

At the end of the Road to the Isles, where the West Highland railway line reaches its terminus, is the town of Mallaig. Here, among the regular ferries that take passengers to Knoydart as well as the isles of Skye, Rum, Eigg, Muck and Canna, you can take a boat to a tiny settlement called Tarbet: population six.

Looking toward the south Morar hills from the north shore of Loch Morar (Ian Frazer/S)

Tiny is not the word. When disembarking you'll be greeted by a collection of two house-like buildings, an old church and – if you peer through the trees on the left side of the bay – the ornate house of theatre impresario Sir Cameron Mackintosh, who has used it as a bolthole since 1994. While the Mackintosh estate may be impressive, it's the church that has the most fascinating background. At present the building sits empty, but peek through the windows and you'll spy old bunk beds, mugs on tables, magazines and books – all the signs of an old hostel. And that's exactly what this place once was. Had you visited before September 2013, you'd have been greeted by Frank Conway, an ex-coalminer from Fife, who believed that bunkhouses should be run as they were when he was young: 'Always ready and willing to take a traveller in need'. Frank would not allow bookings: if you turned up there would always be room, and he insisted on charging only £2 per night for a bed. Google his name and you will find endless tales of his hospitality, stories, singing, whisky, insults and a wealth of love and respect for this upstanding host. Since he passed away, the accommodation is no longer available, but do stop to pay your respects before continuing to the loch and pitching your tent.

You're unlikely to spy Morag on your escapade to this huge loch, which was formed millions of years ago by glacial erosion over a fault line. But its deep waters harbour other aquatic life, including brown trout, Arctic char, Atlantic salmon and eel. Scan the shoreline for otters, and check the skies for golden or white-tailed eagles, both of which regularly overfly the area.

On your walk out the next day keep your eyes peeled for the ruins of Brinacory – another former hamlet – and of Inverbeg Chapel, a great spot for lunch. The idea of retreating to live in this remote place will consume your imagination for the entire walk to the train station and your whistle-stop return to Mallaig on the train. Tickets please.

Look out for otters along the shore (Elliot Neep/FLPA)

HERE'S THE PLAN
DAY 1

1 After stocking up on supplies in Mallaig, take the ferry to Tarbet. It takes about 40 minutes and usually departs at around midday.

2 On arrival at the jetty you'll have landed in the heart of the Mackintosh estate – note his ornate house on the left side of the bay. Check out the former church, once a bunkhouse run by the imitable Frank Conway until he passed away in 2013. Look back from here over to the Knoydart Peninsula then, turning your back on the water, head uphill on the wide and well-defined track. It's a steep but quick pull to the highest point, from where you start to descend once more.

3 Be sure to make a right where the path forks so as not to go to the other jetty. From here continue on the path. Soon you'll reach the house at Swordland. The path undulates as it traverses the coastline, from high above it to down beside the water's edge. Continue on the track until you reach the jutting section of land at Sròn Ghaothar: the perfect place for a camp. With two little sand spits on either side and commanding views both up and down the loch, this is a great place to pitch and watch the waves for signs of Morag. Fall asleep to the sound of the water lapping around you on three sides.

⚊ The ferry will drop walkers at Tarbet

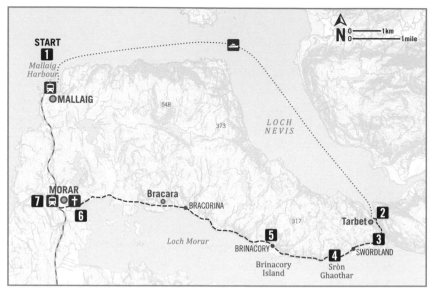

DAY 2

4 Continue on the path and you will come to Brinacory, the site of an old hamlet, where the shell of the schoolhouse and other homesteads still stand amongst the trees.

5 Go further still and you will, at length, come to a much wider track and the ruins of the Inverbeg Chapel. It's hard to believe now but this used to be quite the meeting point on a Sunday. From here on out the track becomes steadily better defined until you reach Bracara and a full tarmac road. You're now on this undulating highway for 4km, but luckily it's a fairly quiet one so not unpleasant. Keep on until the road forks, at which point you turn right.

6 You'll first pass the new church before reaching the main road. Turn right onto the road and follow it for a few hundred metres until you reach the railway line. The station will be on your right.

7 Catch the train from Morar Station back to Mallaig, knowing you've completed a perfect round trip.

TOP TIP It's certainly possible to tackle this weekend in reverse if you'd rather. Just remember that the ferry leaves Tarbet at a set time, and that it's vital to book it to secure a space. And don't forget to take your midge repellent, no matter what.

TOP A perfect camp spot above Loch Morar
CENTRE Catching the train back to Mallaig
BOTTOM Tracing the loch to the remains of Inverbeg Chapel

NUTS AND BOLTS

PRE-TRIP There's nowhere to get supplies on the way so stock up in Mallaig, where you'll find a Co-op and a Spar. Visit Mallaig train station before you leave, to double-check the train times from Morar. There are normally only three or four a day, with long waits in between, so make sure you time it right. Miss one and you could always walk the last 5km on the road, although it may be tough on the feet. Make sure you book your ferry in advance: call one of the companies or pop into the offices at Mallaig Harbour.

PUBLIC TRANSPORT Two ferry services are available. Knoydart Ferry (👆 www. knoydartferry.com), which operates the official Mallaig to Inverie service, also does a 13.20 stop at Tarbet daily during the summer; prices from £20. If no ferry is running they will usually make you a reasonable offer for a private transfer; it's worth enquiring pre-trip. The other option is Western Isles Cruises (👆 westernislescruises.co.uk), who run scheduled and private transfers from Mallaig. Enquire beforehand and you may get a competitive deal. The West Highland train (👆 www.nationalrail.co.uk) runs three times daily in summer and less often during the rest of the year, with prices from £4.40 one-way.

WHEN TO GO Owing to the increased frequency of the trains and ferries, this weekend is best done in the late spring or over summer. It may be possible all year,

but you will need first to check on the ferries and trains. Be warned, though, that midges will be an issue in summer. Take plenty of repellent and consider a midge face-net for when in camp.

IF YOU DON'T FANCY THE WILD CAMP? At present camping is the only option. There are reports that Mackintosh is planning to open another hostel or B&B at Tarbet. Nothing is yet confirmed, but it's worth monitoring.

SHORT OF TIME? The whole journey can be done as a long day. If so, you should pre-book the Tarbet to Mallaig ferry and do the walk in reverse. Be sure to get an early train to Morar, though, as you don't want miss the only boat, which leaves at 15.00 from Tarbet jetty.

TIME TO SPARE? You can enjoy the ultimate multi-day wilderness experience by combining this walk with the crossing of Knoydart, across Loch Nevis. This will probably save you money on ferry costs. Or walk between the two if you have the time and energy.

MORE INFO

Journey to Mallaig 🖱 www.road-to-the-isles.org.uk
Local 🖱 www.mallaigheritage.org.uk
Scotland 🖱 www.visitscotland.com

Look west from Mallaig for a view of the Isle of Eigg (John A Cameron/S)

18 SKYE'S THE LIMIT

HIKE BENEATH THE WILD CUILLINS TO A LONELY BOTHY AND A BEACH WITH A VIEW ON SKYE, WESTERN ISLES

WHERE	Isle of Skye, Scotland
DURATION	2 nights, 3 days
START/FINISH	Kilmarie lay-by 📍 NG545172
MAPS	OS Landranger (1:50,000) 32; OS Explorer (1:25,000) 411

They say that if you ever want to test your mettle as a mountain-goer in the UK – and discover just how far you'll go to prove your love for the high and spiky places – then you have to head for Skye. For this island, the biggest of the Inner Hebrides, is home to the legendary Black Cuillins.

You'll see them long before you arrive. Drive up the eponymous Road to the Isles and you can't miss them: a bristling ridge of spires and buttresses that seem to rise, on many a day, above the clouds. Made from a mix of igneous rock in the form of climber-friendly rough and grippy gabbro, and its antithesis, the slippery (especially when wet) and more crumbly basalt, they glisten an ominous black in certain lights – like the evil baddy's castle in a children's cartoon.

> **" A SECRET PASSAGEWAY TO A REMOTE AND PERFECTLY SITED BEACH AND BOTHY "**

At first sight, the thought of trying to climb the Black Cuillins' blade-like summits should, if you have even an ounce of common sense, strike a stomach-churning fear into you. To give you some idea, a full ridge crossing involves 12 summits, of which one – the aptly named Inaccessible Pinnacle – is a Moderate-graded rock climb that even Sir Hugh Munro, he who classified most of Scotland's peaks, couldn't stomach, and which should take a good walker 12–15 hours, with no water source along the way. From that point, it is said, you will know one way or the other: that either you'll attempt to conquer them all, or you'll swear off Alpine peaks for life.

Thankfully, there is an equally exciting and less hazardous adventure awaiting you on this, the most accessible of all Scotland's islands. Even better, it affords some of the best views of the mighty Cuillin without you ever having to set foot on them. Maintained by the John Muir Trust is the wild and can't-believe-how-truly-gobsmackingly-good-this-view-is area of Camasunary. Ostensibly guarded by the peaks of Blaven, Sgurr na Stri and their bigger Cuillin brothers, the route begins just outside the tiny hamlet of Kilmarie. It starts off unassumingly, between two grassy fields, and it's easy to question just where on earth these so-called great mountains are hiding. But then you reach Am Mam. Here the route takes what feels like a secret passageway to a remote and perfectly sited beach and bothy.

Mountain and sea combine in spectacular fashion at Camasunary. Whether bothying or camping, you'll have a night to remember, watching the sun setting over the isles of Eigg and Rum. Keep an eye out for wildlife: you may spot a sea eagle soaring overhead, a foraging otter along the shore or, during summer, even a basking shark or minke whale out in the bay.

The next day you head on up to Sligachan, Skye's crossroads, where the three roads – to Portree, Dunvegan and Broadford – all meet. Here, after drinking in the views of the mountains, you'll be able to sample one of the local ales from the onsite microbreweries at a hotel that has sat here since the early 1830s.

Before you turn and head back for your start point on the final day, be sure to have your morning wash in the water at Sligachan. Legend has it that if you run your face in its flow for seven seconds you will be rewarded with eternal beauty. That, sadly, may not work for everyone, but one thing's guaranteed: the beauty of this corner of Skye will be etched on your mind forever.

HERE'S THE PLAN
DAY 1

1 From the parking lay-by at Kilmarie cross the road and pass through the gate on the footpath signposted for Sligachan. It's a stony but wide and clear track, with grassy fields on both sides. Although on the map it looks fairly straight, tracking roughly northwest, shortly after crossing the river it begins to zigzag uphill, gaining height rapidly as you climb the lower flanks of Slat Bheinn. Before long the gradient relents and a flattened stroll at the bealach will have you wondering where they keep the views – until you turn a corner and begin snaking in a more northerly

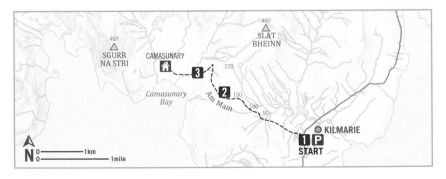

direction, at which point the epic views down to Camasunary Bay, over to Sgurr na Stri and the infamous Black Cuillins beyond, greet you. Have your camera ready.

2 Continue as the track now begins to descend toward the waterfalls. Be sure to stick to it where it swings round to bear momentarily south, before heading more west, bringing you down to the estate.

3 At this point the route to Sligachan that you'll take the next day is more obvious, veering off to your right. But for now continue straight, through the long grass. It will probably be boggy so make a line towards the beach and you'll soon pick up the solid ground and a grassy path that will lead you west to the bothy. With five 'bedrooms' and two living rooms/kitchens, there's plenty of room in Camasunary, though it is perhaps a little tired. Choose yours but don't forget to head out to the beach. Here you may be lucky enough to find some driftwood for the fire (though take your own fuel as this is not guaranteed). There is no better place than this sandy patch, in the heart of Skye's wild mountains, from which to watch the sunset. A new bothy at Camasunary is set to open in summer 2015, 1km east of the existing one. It will sleep around 15 people (with a maximum group size of six). Check the MBA website for up-to-date information and in the meantime always take a tent or bivvy as an alternative.

TOP Leaving Kilmarie
BOTTOM Camasunary bothy; Signpost to Camasunary

DAY 2

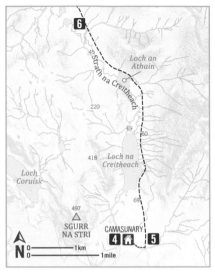

4 Congratulations! You've just woken up in one of the most spectacular bays in Scotland. After enjoying your breakfast, retrace your steps along the grassy path above the beach and this time, shortly after the stone wall of the estate, turn left. Once you've made it over the grass to the wider track, the way forward is obvious. But, if in doubt, shortly after the last building an old ruin carries the word 'Sligachan' in large white emulsion, and a helpful arrow.

5 Follow the path and after just over 1km you will reach the shores of Loch na Creitheach, the beautiful mountains rising up as craggy giants either side of you. Continue north along the path, which will be joined by another before you reach the loch head. You'll pass another, smaller loch on your left – Loch an Athain – before swinging slightly northwest.

Glamaig (Sgurr Mhairi) mountain from Sligachan on the Isle of Skye (Targn Pleiades/S)

6 Here, the path from Loch Coruisk – an even wilder place below the Cuillin Ridge (though accessible by boat from Elgol if you fancy it for another day) – joins your path and is marked by a large cairn. Continue north, beneath the slopes of Marsco. From this point the going gets quite boggy, as you cross several streams. You'll see the white glimmer of the Sligachan Hotel way before you reach it. Persevere. Eventually the rough path becomes more defined and pitched, until you meet a gate in the fence. Pass through and soon you'll reach the stone bridge (built by Thomas Telford himself). Cross the road and head into the Sligachan Hotel for a well-earned drink and cooked meal. Whether staying in the luxury of the hotel or camping in their site across the road, you're sure for a great night in a place designed for sharing mountain adventures.

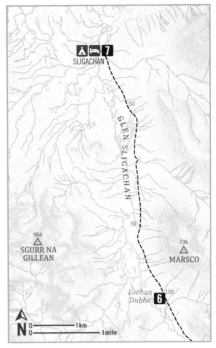

DAY 3

7 If the weather behaves, you'll wake in the morning to views of the legendary Cuillin. If so, be sure to take lots of photos, as they often fail to show. Today you will retrace your steps from the last two days, first with your stroll down Glen Sligachan. The only tweak in the route you may consider is at the fork in the path near the head of Loch na Creitheach, when you could take the left path, which climbs steadily and eventually joins the route up and over Am Mam's shoulder, then follows your footsteps back to Kilmarie.

TOP TIP If planning to stay at the bothy it's worth carrying in your own fuel (eg: a small bag of coal). The going is not too hard from Kilmarie, and you can take your time, knowing that after the first 2km it's downhill. It's worth it to be assured of a warm night.

NUTS AND BOLTS

PRE-TRIP Make sure you pick up supplies in Broadford, which has the last supermarket (a Co-op behind the BP garage) before Kilmarie. Book in advance (www. sligachan.co.uk) if you plan to stay at the Sligachan Hotel. Reservations are not required for camping.

PUBLIC TRANSPORT It is possible to do this walk via bus. Stagecoach number 55 stops in Kilmarie (runs from Kyle of Lochalsh on the mainland and calls at Broadford). If you only want to do the walk one-way, then you can pick up the 917, 52 or 155 at Sligachan and either return to Broadford to catch the bus back to Kilmarie or continue to the mainland and beyond.

WHEN TO GO A visit to Camasunary can be enjoyed year-round. Spring and autumn are good options for a crowd-free visit, when the mountains are a beautiful colour and the midges less aggressive than in mid summer. The weather on Skye is variable at any season so make sure you go prepared.

IF YOU DON'T FANCY THE BOTHY? The bothy can and does get crowded. A new bothy is planned for summer 2015. Either way, the ground outside is perfectly flat and many people opt for a wild camp instead.

SHORT OF TIME? If you want to experience the beauty of the bothy location but stay only one night you could simply walk in from Kilmarie and cut out the section to Sligachan. Or do the walk one-way, using buses (see Public Transport, above).

TIME TO SPARE? This part of the coastline is littered with idyllic wild camp spots to discover. Loch Coruisk is a great option and, if you're up for the climb, the view of the Cuillin Ridge from atop Sgurr na Stri is world class.

MORE INFO

Up-to-date bothy conditions www.mountainbothies.org.uk

A gripping tale of staying at the bothy in 1982 when a plane crashed on the hill behind it http://heavywhalley.wordpress.com (post on 4/12/12)

Local www.skye.co.uk

Scotland www.visitscotland.com

Loch Coruisk, below the Cuillin mountains on the Isle of Skye (N Mrtgh/S)

WHERE	Glen Coe, Scotland
DURATION	1 night, 2 days
START/FINISH	Parking lay-by at Altnafeadh 📍 NN220563
MAPS	OS Landranger (1:50,000) 41; OS Explorer (1:25,000) 384

Mountains become icons for a reason. Usually, it boils down to height or notoriety. Take Everest (the world's highest) and K2 (arguably its deadliest): both are easy to picture and trigger an immediate reaction as soon as you hear their names. In the UK we have our fair share of icons. The highest peaks in England, Wales and Scotland – Scafell Pike, Snowdon and Ben Nevis, respectively – are well known even to non-mountain lovers. But there are other peaks that have acquired an iconic status among us outdoor lovers less for their fame or reputation and more for their shape.

19 BED DOWN ON THE BUCKLE

SLEEP ON THE SUMMIT OF ONE OF SCOTLAND'S MOST ICONIC MOUNTAINS AT BUCHAILLE ETIVE MOR, GLEN COE

In Wales, the promontory that takes this prize is undoubtedly Tryfan – the spiky ridge that resembles the open jaws of a prehistoric monster. In England the same award, in my humble opinion, would have to be reserved for Great Gable, the hulking mass that sits at the foot of Wast Water. When it comes to Scotland there are many contenders: An Teallach – a true rock star among mountains, steadfastly

> **A DELICIOUSLY CONICAL MOUNTAIN THAT GREETS ALL TRAVELLERS UP THIS WESTERN EDGE OF SCOTLAND**

guarded by its bristling entourage of towers; Skye's Cuillin Ridge – a dark volcanic collection of spires and buttresses that inspires both fear and desire in many a mountaineer; Slioch – an isolated peak with a summit that appears, at least at first, impossibly sharp. But for me, among all these and many more, the most iconic is found in Glen Coe.

Buchaille Etive Mor – 'the great herdsman of Etive' – is a deliciously conical mountain that greets all travellers up this western edge of Scotland,

Buchaille Etive Mor mountain – AKA 'The Buckle' (Andrew West/S)

her granite pillars hanging below the summit like a thorny necklace, the scree glinting down her front like pewter diamonds. Of course you have to catch her from the right angle: come at her wrong, and this pyramidal princess becomes nothing more than a rolling rump of grass and scree. The best view of The Buckle (as she is affectionately nicknamed) is from the Kings House pub, where red deer roam the grounds and you can catch her in all her symmetrical glory.

Climbing this mountain for a summit sleep is of course a wholly different prospect. After gazing at your goal from the road, it's far easier – in summer at least – to nip up by an altogether less shapely route. But once at the col, and then the summit, you will, with luck, have earned a stunning bedtime panorama that is usually reserved for the local golden eagles. Ben Nevis and its kidney bean-shaped plateau looms to the north; the rest of the mountain chain of Buchaille Etive Mor and the Black Mount lies to the southwest and southeast (reminding you that this first summit visible from the road is but one point on a sprawling mountaintop); and the vast empty expanse of the bewitching Rannoch Moor stretches out to the east.

For the perfect summit sleep you need little more than good weather and a great sleeping and bivvy bag. When you wake up to that exquisite vista in the morning, as sunrise tinges the dark hills with an orange blush, remind yourself that it has cost you nothing to spend the night on this mountain mattress. And then pinch yourself: no, you're not dreaming.

A golden eagle keeps an eye out for prey (Mark Caunt/S) ▲

HERE'S THE PLAN
DAY 1

1 Leaving the lay-by at Altnafeadh, head south along the wide track as it crosses the River Coupall via a bridge. Bear to the right and you'll soon pass Lagangarbh Hut. Owned by the National Trust For Scotland, this former crofter's home has been used and maintained by the Scottish Mountaineering Club since 1946. (Rumour has it that one of the bunks inside has a million-dollar view of the Buchaille.)

2 Shortly after passing the hut, the path divides. Unless you have a head for heights (not to mention a rope and helmets), you will need to take the right fork, heading up Coire na Tulaich. This leads over rocky ground up and into the heart of the mountain.

3 On the OS map the path appears to peter out around the 700m mark. Not to worry: the way up should be obvious, thanks to the footfall of those who have been before you. It is very steep, though, with loose scree, so care is needed. This is the well-known blackspot for winter avalanches,

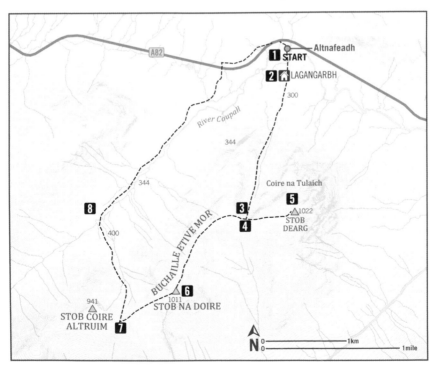

TOP Red deer beneath The Buckle ⚠
BOTTOM Walking from Stob Dearg, Ben Nevis in the distance

when climbing it is not advised. Soon you'll emerge onto the col between your goal, Stob Dearg, and the subsidiary nameless mound at 902m.

4 From here you turn left to follow the broad and boulder-strewn ridge up to the summit of Stob Dearg, the highest point on the Buchaille and, all being well, your bed for the night. At the summit take a deep breath and settle in your bivvy to enjoy the views; they're yours for the night. If you're lucky, you may see the setting or rising sun cast the shadow of the mountain over Rannoch Moor below.

DAY 2

5 If you're short on time then simply retrace your steps down to the car. Otherwise, if the weather is good and time is on your side, then try this alternative descent: retrace your steps to the col but this time continue along the ridge, first up to the subsidiary summit at 902m and then bearing left in a southeasterly direction – first descending slightly before climbing again to the summit of Stob na Doire, crossing large slabs of flat rock.

6 After enjoying more views from here, continue along the ridge, taking care to follow its curves (do not descend into the wrong valley – easily done in bad weather), but once again descending, before climbing towards the unnamed summit at 860m.

7 Munro-baggers may be tempted to continue along the ridge from this point to bag the second Munro on the Buchaille: Stob na Bròige. To do this, you'll need to ascend Stob Coire Altruim as it undulates. Either way, the route down comes after this point. A steep but mainly grassy path heading north will take you down Coire Altruim and into the glen below. Keep to the west side of the Allt Coire Altrium as you descend.

8 Once at the bottom you'll need to cross the stream and turn right to follow the path through Lairig Gartain, keeping to the north side of the River Coupall that cuts through it. It can become saturated after heavy rain, so gaiters are useful. You will eventually arrive at the A82. Turn right onto it and follow the road back to your car – watching out for the fast-moving traffic as you go. Once back in your vehicle, don't forget to take one last look at the Buchaille and remind yourself: I slept up there last night!

TOP TIP Summit sleeps are not pleasant in bad weather so check the conditions before you go and don't be afraid to change your plans. Having a plan B is always sensible: the mountains will be there another day.

NUTS AND BOLTS

SLEEPING ON A SUMMIT Bear in mind that summit sleeps, including this one, often mean no easy access to water. You need to be self-sufficient: take enough water not only for drinking but also cooking, and for any hot drinks you might want to lull you to sleep or wake you in the morning. Summits can be rocky, so take a good camping mat — and, if it's inflatable/self-inflating, a repair kit. Sitting around up high can get cold so take plenty of warm, insulating layers and lots of food and treats (eg: chocolate, hot drink sachets). Also keep the use of your headtorch/camera flash to a minimum: you don't want to alarm a passer-by who sees your lights and thinks someone needs help. Take a bivvy bag rather than a tent if possible: that way you're more likely to be woken by the sunrise. And enjoy!

PRE-TRIP If you think you'll arrive too late for a summit sleep, two well-established mountaineering establishments offer accommodation: The Kings House Hotel (🖰 www.kingshousehotel.co.uk) gets the best view of Buchaille Etive Mor and also has its regular antler-clad visitors. The other option is the Clachaig Inn (🖰 www.clachaig.com). Don't be fooled by the occasional coach party; this is the meeting place for hill-goers to share their tales of near-misses and must-climb peaks. The haggis, neeps and tatties (with a great vegetarian version also offered) are excellent. It's also good choice for a post-summit sleep. If you want a little more rugged luxury then you can apply to sleep at the Lagangarbh Hut (🖰 www.smc.org.uk/huts/lagangarbh), as mentioned in Step 1 (see page 169).

PUBLIC TRANSPORT Scottish City Link (🖰 www.citylink.co.uk), lines 914, 915 and 916, runs a service every three hours from Fort William to the King's House Hotel.

WHEN TO GO Summer is the best season. In winter the ascent/descent route described here often has a high avalanche risk and is not recommended even with the proper equipment. In summer, as you'll be climbing up when others are coming down, you won't have to deal with crowds, and at this height the breeze helps keep midges at bay.

IF YOU DON'T FANCY THE SUMMIT SLEEP? A good alternative is the col that you reach before pulling up to the summit or the subsidiary peak at 902m where there is some water. You could also just tackle the walk by day and then stay in one of the pubs named above.

SHORT OF TIME? You needn't go far to find an iconic peak to lay your head on. Why not try a night under the stars on your local hilly hero, no matter where it is. Same rules apply: go prepared, travel light, go late and leave early. Above all, wait for good weather and enjoy the experience.

TIME TO SPARE? As mentioned, the 'summit' of the Buchaille is a sprawling mass of contours. You may decide to explore further, then camp lower down for a second night. Just make sure the route you take is within your capabilities: there are lots of climbs on Buchaille Etive Mor, so don't ever climb up what you can't climb down.

MORE INFO
Glencoe ☗ www.glencoe-nts.org.uk
Lagangarbh Hut bookings ☗ www.smc.org.uk/huts/lagangarbh
Scotland info ☗ www.visitscotland.com

Lagangarbh Hut sits beneath The Buckle

WHERE	Glen Coe, Scotland
DURATION	2 days, 1 night
START	Rannoch Station 📍 NN423579
FINISH	Spean Bridge 📍 NN221814
MAPS	OS Landranger (1:50,000) 42, 41;
	OS Explorer (1:25,000) 385, 392

F ormed by an enormous slow-moving glacier during the last ice age, over 10,000 years ago, Rannoch is a vast expanse of raw, unspoilt landscape that stretches over hundreds of acres north and west from the station that shares its name. Sitting at around 300m above sea level, unlike any other UK moorland, this is not a simple raised plateau but a gouged-out granite bowl, surrounded by soaring peaks in every direction. And this means that whenever it rains, the bowl fills up with water running off the hills, transforming it into a mosaic of lochs, blanket bogs, peat hags and streams that trickle and meander among the rocky promontories.

20 MOOR THAN MEETS THE EYE

HIKE THROUGH BOGS, PEAKS AND GHOSTS
TO REACH A WILD BOTHY ON RANNOCH MOOR, GLEN COE

Unsurprisingly, these conditions make Rannoch fairly inaccessible. The B846 road may weave along its edges, tantalising you with glimpses of its wild heart, but no road will take you into its depths. Only a train can do that. Built by the determined Victorians, the railway line slices across the barren lands, floating in places on brushwood rafts with up to 6m of bog lurking below. Once off the train, it's time to explore only on foot.

> **ON RANNOCH, THE LANDSCAPE DEFINITELY SHOWS US WHO IS BOSS**

From the station, an old drovers' road will lead you across Rannoch, in the footsteps of the bygone cattle herders who once led their stock through the moor. It would have been hard-going for them, but the only way to take their merchandise south or east to market. Now, handily, those well-worn tracks offer a relatively straightforward passageway among the rough mountains.

The journey may not always be easy, but there are plenty of sights along the way. To the west, the conical giant of Buchaille Etive Mor (literally 'the

Lone tree on Rannoch Moor, Glen Coe (Targn Pleiades/S)

shepherd who guards the moor') will greet you, if you're lucky enough to have clear skies. Next will come several stream crossings through an increasingly saturated grassy carpet, testing both your nerve and your balancing skills.

Further in, you'll hit the ruins of Corrour Old Lodge, formerly the highest shooting lodge in Scotland. Once the base for the moneyed few, this building eventually lost favour with the hunting crowd, especially when a more modern structure was built nearer the loch. At the turn of the 20th century it was run as a sanatorium, before being abandoned and de-roofed in the 1930s. Now merely a network of crumbling corridors, empty window frames and decaying brickwork, it must in its heyday have been an imposing sight: the grey slabs towering above the landscape, with their bold right angles and straight edges, issuing a defiant manmade challenge to the wild moor. Today nature has begun to reclaim it: slick green slime covers parts of the walls, a mossy carpet conceals fallen stone and the sky is now the ceiling. On Rannoch, the landscape definitely shows us who is boss.

Further on, where the shores of Loch Ossian come into view, stands Peter's Rock. This innocuous-looking lump of stone is a memorial to a man called Peter Trowell, former warden of nearby Loch Ossian Youth Hostel, owned and run by the Scottish Youth Hostels Association (SYHA). He remained in the building over the winter in 1978 to undertake some refurbishment, but disappeared. No-one knew what had happened to him. When the loch thawed, several weeks later, his body was found in the water. It's thought that he must have fallen in while tending to something on the shore or jetty, but as he was alone, the truth remains a mystery.

As well as its physical landmarks, the area also comes with numerous legends. Ghosts are said to haunt Rannoch, as are witches that morph into vampires when you kill them. Worst of all is the Cu Saeng, a monster said to be so horrific that even a glimpse of it would kill you. It may thus be with such apparitions in mind that you follow the path further to Corrour Station and the Lodge and Restaurant. Back in Victorian times, there was no such sanctuary but only small emergency shacks beside the tracks, where passengers could seek refuge if the train broke down. In the depths of winter, due to the altitude, temperatures here can plummet and deep snow can carpet the ground. If arriving during that season, this can be the perfect point to warm up.

From this point, the journey takes on a different character. It's a railside track to Loch Treig, where the deep bogs are often overcome with the help of old wooden sleepers. Finally the huge stretch of water – at first glance, appearing far too big to be merely a loch – appears ahead. Here, the flanks of steep hills encircle the water.

Today the loch is used as a reservoir, and is dammed at one end for a hydro-electricity project. Before these developments, it was the site of two small communities, Kinlochtrig and Creaguaineach, who hosted key livestock markets – perhaps accounting for the loch's Gaelic name, which translates as 'Loch of Death'. They marked the end of a couple of tracks

(and of life for many animals), and were a place where the drovers could sell, replenish and refresh before taking the long journey home. Neither place exists any longer: both were submerged beneath the dam. Now all that remains are the paths that lead on to the Lairig Leacach valley and Spean Bridge, and the track that brought you here. Follow the path across a rickety bridge and alongside the old hunting lodge and continue, as you still have some way to go.

Eventually the reward of the small bothy will greet you. With water gushing by outside it's an ideal place to relax inside and share stories of your epic walk-in, before taking the much less boggy track out and off to the train station. On my first night in that bothy, I heard another name for this route: the 'thieves' roads', so-called because of the bandits and exiled clansmen who would hide out here and rob unsuspecting victims. I laughed at how the biggest threat today is merely the boggy ground and midges.

HERE'S THE PLAN
DAY 1

1 Take the train to Rannoch Station: this departs from Glasgow Queen Street Station, a short walk from Glasgow Central. From the station, follow the B846 road east away from the tracks. After about 1.5km you'll see a sign for a footpath on your left. Take this and begin your track onto the moorland.

Red deer stag: the monarch of the glen (Targn Pleiades/S) ⛰

2 Follow the track as it veers first northwest then north, taking care not to detour right at the fork (keep left; if you hit the lochan you've gone too far). A bridge will take you over the Allt Eigheach. From here the track may become less defined. After about 500m the track forks again. Take the left fork so that you no longer trace the edge of the river, keeping the peak of Carn Dearg to your right and the moorland to your left. You'll pass Old Corrour Lodge on your way.

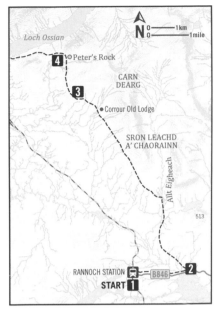

3 After the lodge, the path forks again. This time take the path on the right, keeping above the moorland on the lower flanks of the hill. Within the next 2km you'll reach Peter's Rock.

4 Turn left as the track divides, now heading roughly west, with Loch Ossian on your right. As you reach the end of the loch you'll see a hostel, with solar panels and wind turbines outside. Here, bear right to emerge onto a wide track/road. Turn left on this and follow it southwest until you reach Corrour Station and the railway track.

A Corrour summit

5 If you're not staying the night here it's still a good place for a break. (It's worth noting that during the daytime the restaurant is only open to residents.) To continue, safely cross the railway track then turn right onto the track that

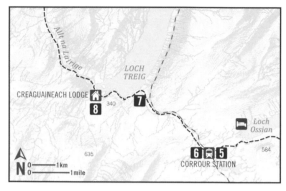

bears roughly northwest, tracing the railway track.

6 Keep the railway track on your right the whole way down to Loch Treig. There is also a river on your right. Where the path divides to pass under the tracks, keep straight on. The track becomes wider and will lead you down to the loch.

7 With the loch in front of you, turn left, crossing the bridges until you get to Creaguaineach Lodge. From here it's about another 6km to the bothy. This is a good wild camp spot if you run out of time.

8 Leave the lodge and continue on the path – which can become very faint in places – making sure you keep to the left of Easan Dubh (river). Follow the path, heading roughly north, below the flanks of Meall Mor, past the waterfalls of Allt na Lairige until, finally, you reach the small bothy.

Lairig Leacach bothy ▲

TOPTIP The hotel in Corrour Station is a great option for those who don't fancy a bothy/wild camp, or who'd like to break the trip into smaller sections. Either way, take a photograph here: it's the famous station from the 1995 film *Trainspotting*.

DAY 2

9 Leaving the bothy, you have a much shorter day ahead of you. From here the path becomes more of an obvious track again and weaves beneath the peaks, descending as it goes. You'll pass under some forest at The Lairig and may spy parts of the dismantled railway and former bridge buttresses on either side.

10 Continue on the path. Don't be tempted to detour through the forest, which is like a maze. You'll reach the minor road at Coire Choille Farm. Turn left onto it and follow it for about 3.5km back into Spean Bridge and your train home.

NUTS AND BOLTS

PRE-TRIP There's nowhere to pick up supplies at Rannoch Station, so make sure you stock up first. Spean Bridge has a couple of convenience stores, but for a proper shop you'll need to head to Fort William where there is a supermarket right by the train station. Unless you're already in Scotland, getting to Rannoch can take a while so this weekend journey is best done via train. If you're coming from London (or have easy access to Watford Junction, Crewe or Preston), a good option is the Caledonian Sleeper, which runs from Euston Station to Fort William on Friday night. This stops directly at Rannoch Station. You'll arrive first thing Saturday morning, feeling refreshed and ready to tackle your adventure straight from the train. And you've not lost any time getting here. On the return journey, you can take the sleeper from Spean Bridge (or Corrour if you decide to truncate the trip) on Sunday night – there's no service on Saturday – and arrive ready for work on Monday morning. Genius! Make sure to book the sleeper well in advance to get the cheapest tickets and/or reserve a sleeper berth, especially if travelling during school holidays.

PUBLIC TRANSPORT Trains make doing this route quite straightforward as they connect both the start and end – far preferable to messing around with two cars. Trains run thrice daily (the Scotrail Sprinter) between Spean Bridge and Rannoch. They stop at Corrour Station, which is a good escape route for those wanting to shorten the experience by finishing after the main Rannoch section, or those who only want to start there and complete the section with the bothy.

WHEN TO GO As with most of Scotland, the weather is a serious consideration. Do this route in winter and you may need crampons due to the ice but you'll be rewarded with views of the peaks caked in white; in summer you may get plagued by midges – courtesy of the bogs – but the (with luck) warm weather may make conditions drier and the going easier. Spring and autumn are your best chance of mild weather and fewer midges, but the main thing you should be watching for before your trip is rain. Go straight after a week or two of rain and parts of the bog may be impassable. Gaiters are a must year round and walking poles are recommended – even if used only to test the depth of the sometimes deceptively innocuous-looking puddles.

IF YOU DON'T FANCY THE BOTHY?
There are many good accommodation alternatives on this route. For a shorter first day, a wild camp at the decaying ruins of Corrour Old Lodge makes for an atmospheric evening. For a quirky stopover without canvas, try Corrour Station House, which is now a lodge and restaurant (Closed Tuesdays year round and Mondays Oct–Mar). For greener credentials, try the SYHA eco-hostel on Loch Ossian just before the station, which is committed to harnessing renewable energy and using composting toilets (open Mar–Oct; limited dates outside those months – check first). Loch Treig offers a supreme wild camp spot, as does most of the land between it and the bothy, if it's not been raining too much.

SHORT OF TIME?
Easy. Either start at Rannoch and take the train back from Corrour – either including a wild camp *en route* or doing it in a single day. Or start at Corrour and do the walk at Spean Bridge, with or without the stay in the bothy.

TIME TO SPARE?
This is another route with multiple options for extensions. Fancy gaining some height? Try climbing the peaks up near Lairig Leacach. Want to take more time? Break the trip down into smaller days with more stops on the way to submerge yourself deeper in the experience. Get out your map and start planning.

MORE INFO
Up-to-date bothy conditions www.mountainbothies.org.uk
Corrour Station House www.corrour-station-house-restaurant.co.uk
Loch Ossian Hostel www.syha.org.uk
Train times and tickets www.nationalrail.co.uk and www.scotrail.co.uk

Steam train arriving at Corrour Station (Michal Lazor/S)

21 BETWEEN A ROCK AND A HARD PLACE

SLEEP UNDER A BOULDER IN
A PROPER MOUNTAIN HINTERLAND, CAIRNGORMS

WHERE	Shelter Stone, Cairngorms, Scotland
DURATION	1 night, 2 days
START/FINISH	Cairn Gorm Mountain Ski Centre car park ♥ NH989060
MAPS	OS Landranger (1:50,000) 36; OS Explorer (1:25,000) 403

Aviemore will easily have you fooled. Shortly after turning off the A9, you'll be greeted by clusters of Swiss-style chalets, outdoor boutiques and whisky-stocked hotels with roaring fires and home comforts. In winter it attracts skiers and snowboarders from miles around to its powder-rich slopes. There are ski lifts and even a funicular railway (the highest in the UK) that will take you up to within a few metres of the summit of Cairn Gorm, the 1,245m peak that shares its name. It's easy to write off this part of the Highlands as a tourist trap and a soft touch. But some of us know better.

Sure, the car park where you start will probably be busy. Go in summer and there will be coachloads of tourists waiting to take the train up the mountain. But everything will make sense soon. As you begin your ascent on the path (walkers are not allowed to use the train to access the peak; those on the train aren't allowed past the viewing level by the station), you may question how wild this trip actually is, but then you'll veer off on a fainter track away from the funicular, climb up to the 1,141m mark and suddenly see laid out before you in 3D all the clusters of contours you saw on an OS, forming a seemingly limitless blanket of peaks. These are mountains with a capital 'M': giants that can catch out even the best-equipped mountaineers. Care is definitely needed.

> **THESE ARE MOUNTAINS WITH A CAPITAL 'M'. A SPRAWLING MASS OF GIANTS THAT CAN CATCH OUT EVEN THE MOST WELL-EQUIPPED MOUNTAINEERS**

Once you've caught your breath, you'll find you've left the crowds well behind. Soon you descend into a valley where the giant cliff-faces loom ahead – vertical slabs that look as though they belong in the Alps. As you descend further, they seem to grow taller still, shrinking you to ant-like stature.

The sparkling water of Loch A'an will greet you at the valley's basin and you'll skirt its edge, heading towards your goal: the Shelter Stone. Marked on the OS map, this is essentially a giant boulder that some centuries ago sheared off from the peaks above. But it is more than just a boulder: resting on other smaller boulders, it hides a sunken chamber underneath. And this makes one cool place to spend a night.

◄ Hunkering down under the Shelter Stone

Sleeping here, you are technically sleeping under an enormous, 1,300-tonne lump of granite. It may sound scary, but once there you'll see how – over the years – visitors have worked hard to make the chamber watertight, with a makeshift wall built up all around its edges, filling in gaps between the boulders to create a cosy place in which to spend the night. The entrance has been carefully arranged to resemble a door frame, through which you must enter on your knees.

Inside you will generally find old groundsheets, frayed and torn with use. You should also find a Tupperware box containing a visitors book (but rarely a working pen – so take your own), in which you can record your experience and read about those of other visitors: from climbers nipping in to grab a cup of tea to day-trippers checking out this natural curiosity and members of the local Cairngorm Club, Scotland's oldest mountaineering club, checking up on it. Indeed, legend has it this club formed back in 1887 – or '89, depending upon who you ask – at this very spot.

You'll probably find the remains of a fire here, too, arranged in a mini-alcove at the back. Though the thought might appeal, it's best to resist the temptation, as smoke can gather quickly in this confined space and there's a distinct lack of escape routes should things get out of hand. It's dark inside even when sunny outside, so take a head torch with you whenever you enter.

The path above Loch A'an

The Shelter Stone is what is known in Scotland as a 'howff'. This term describes a variety of natural shelters – anything from rocky overhangs to nooks so sheltered by trees that no tent is needed to keep out the elements. The word is also used to describe a meeting place and even a pub. It is thought to derive from the Old English 'hof', which means 'enclosure'. Temporary shelters like these have been used for many years by Highland workers and climbers as free accommodation in the heart of the mountains.

But don't get too fixated on the Shelter Stone; remember to take some time to gaze out at your surrounds. Wonder at the sunlight glimmering on the surface of the loch, and the silence of being in a valley accessible only by foot. And, as day turns to night, enjoy the stream of stars in a night sky free from light pollution. All this, and you get to go back to work on Monday morning and brag that you've literally been caught between a rock and a hard place.

A Inside the Shelter Stone

HERE'S THE PLAN
DAY 1

1 Leave the car park and take the track that runs to the left of the funicular railway and continues parallel to it for the first 750m. It will pass underneath the tracks, before swinging south and taking you through a couple of switchbacks towards Fiacaill a' Choire Chais.

2 On the second switchback, as the main track turns east towards the ski tow, you'll notice a smaller path climbing up the hillside on your right. Take this and follow it as it continues south. Where it forks, don't be tempted to take the left path as you'll end up back on the main track you left. Instead, follow the ridge spine you're on, as a series of natural steps takes you up through the boulders to the marker stone known as 1,141 (its height in metres).

3 Stop for a minute to enjoy the magnificent views, which can extend over the chain of peaks to Cairn Lochan and beyond. It's from here that you'll really get a sense of just how big and extensive these mountains really are. From the cairn, with your back to the path you just followed up, the summit of Cairn Gorm rising to your left and the ridge along to Stob Coire an t-Sneachda to your right, head straight on to pick up a fainter path down to Corie Raibeirt. You'll lose height immediately, crossing over grassy ground that gets boggy after rain and snow. As you get closer to the river, the path becomes much more defined and steep. Take care as you follow it down. The water of Loch A'an soon appears in front of you, with the summit of Stob Coire Etchachan looming above like a granite giant.

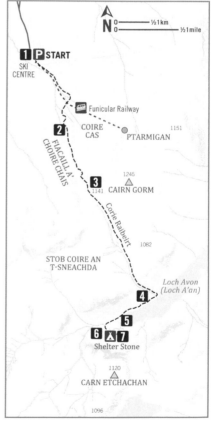

The beach at Loch A'an

4 About 20m from the water's edge, turn right to cross the stream, heading southwest. The water is wide and can be fast-flowing, but there should be ample makeshift stepping stones. Take care, and use walking poles if you have them. There is a higher track and a lower one (closer to the loch edge). I prefer to use the higher one as it's often less boggy, but they meet just over 500m later so either will work.

5 At the beach, the path heads away from the water and up a small incline. Scan the boulder field in front of you: the Shelter Stone is one of the largest boulders there and so fairly easy to spot if you're familiar with it from a photograph (certainly easier than once you're among the boulders). Follow the path to a narrower section of the ford, where it's much easier to cross. Take care, as the ground can be saturated even if it hasn't recently rained.

6 You'll now be heading south on the path as it weaves through the rocks. You'll no doubt spy other, smaller boulders that could serve as a place to sleep but continue until eventually, courtesy of the manmade

TOP TIP Despite the best effort of previous guests, the floor is usually damp inside the Shelter Stone so do take a bivvy bag or good piece of tarp for the ground to stop your sleeping bag getting too wet.

wall outside it, you'll spot the Shelter Stone (which is even marked on the OS map). Duck down to enter. Once inside, it's high enough, near the entrance, for you to sit on a small camping stool. Further in, you can still sit on the floor with no problem. It sleeps four comfortably and six at a push, but if you're very lucky you'll get it to yourself. Sweet dreams.

DAY 2

7 There are other routes that go further into the Cairngorms hinterland, and other paths that will take you out, but the easiest and best way is simply to retrace your footsteps from day 1 and head back to the car, knowing that you've had a proper adventure in one of the best mountain ranges in the UK.

Heading down to Coire Raibeirt

191

NUTS AND BOLTS

PRE-TRIP From hostels to B&Bs, self-catering lodges, campsites and five-star hotels, there are numerous accommodation options if you want to drive up on a Friday and stay the night before your big adventure. If you plan to take the train, Aviemore Station has direct connections to London and all stops in between. This is a 7.5-hour journey with East Coast Trains (📱 www.nationalrail.co.uk). To maximise your time, consider taking the Inverness Scotrail Sleeper from London Euston, Watford, Crewe or Preston on a Friday night (📱 www.scotrail.co.uk). You'll arrive at 07.50, ready to begin your journey to the Shelter Stone. You can then return on Sunday night and be back in time for work on Monday morning. Book the sleeper well in advance to get the cheapest tickets and/or reserve a sleeper berth – especially if travelling during school holidays. If you'd rather take the coach, both Citylink and Stagecoach offer services to the area.

PUBLIC TRANSPORT From Aviemore Station to the start of the walk take the local Stagecoach service number 31 (📱 www.stagecoachbus.com). This goes via Glenmore (so good for the 'Time to spare' option, see page 193) and will drop you off at the Cairn Gorm Mountain Ski Centre car park.

WHEN TO GO As winters vary from year to year, keep a close eye on the forecast, starting at least the week before your planned trip so that you will know what to expect. As a general rule, to avoid the worst of the snow go May–November.

IF YOU DON'T FANCY THE BOULDER? If you don't like the idea of sheltering under tonnes of granite, or you arrive at the Shelter Stone to find other adventurers have beaten you to it, don't despair. There is a great alternative on the shores of Loch A'an. Pitch on the sand, surrounded by the mountain amphitheatre, and enjoy the thought that no-one else can get there without a long walk in.

SHORT OF TIME? You could start early and just see the Shelter Stone without sleeping over. It's still an incredible walk and a great natural feature to explore.

TIME TO SPARE? By the time you've reached the Shelter Stone you're already in the heart of the mountains. You could continue on the path to Loch Etchachan, a great spot to wild camp, and perhaps take in the summit of Ben Macdui. From there you could stay up high, walking to Cairn Lochan to pick up the ridge you left at step 3, and head back to the car. Alternatively if you're after length rather than height, you can retrace your steps to the loch. Then, instead of heading up Coire Raibeirt, follow the path up to The Saddle and follow the Garbh Allt (river) down Strath Nethy to join the wide track that will bring you out by An Lochan Uaine. It's a fair walk from there back to your car, but going via Glenmore Lodge you can take one of the forest tracks onto the road and either catch a bus, put your thumb out for a lift or start walking. Well, you did say you wanted a longer route!

MORE INFO

Cairngorms National Park www.cairngorms.co.uk
Cairngorm Club www.cairngormclub.org.uk
Visit Cairngorms www.visitcairngorms.com. Official site for accommodation, other attractions in the area pre/post trip.
Avalanche conditions www.sais.gov.uk

Snow transforms the Cairngorms into a truly Arctic wilderness.

WHERE	Sutherland, northern Highlands
DURATION	3 days, 2 nights
START/FINISH	Kylestrome car park ♥ NC217345
MAPS	OS Landranger (1:50,000) 15; OS Explorer (1:25,000) 442

The Europeans have got it right. If you've ever been to the Alps you'll know that some of their most famous walking routes are strung between a series of mountain huts – placed, ideally, in prime peak country. These continental huts may, of course, offer a little luxury: beds with mattresses, flushing toilets, the occasional shower and even on-site catering. But we have something even better and, what's more, completely free, with no booking required: bothies. Look at a map of Scotland and you'll soon spot them: those friendly little squares of thick black lines. And there are so many that you can easily string together a Continental-style hut-to-hut adventure right here in the UK.

22 BOTHY TO BOTHY

TAKE A WILD TRAIL BETWEEN TWO REMOTE BOTHIES AND RETURN BY BOAT, SUTHERLAND, NORTHERN HIGHLANDS

One of the best routes is at Kylesku: a remote little fishing hamlet in Scotland's far north, whose cluster of homes and pub traces the edge of Loch Glencoul and Loch Gleann Dubh. These two patches of water converge here to feed into Loch a' Chairn Bhain, which eventually winds its way out to sea. Drive

DON'T BE FOOLED: THIS ROUTE WILL KEEP YOU ON YOUR TOES

the route to the start of this trail and you'll cross over the gloriously modern bridge that joins the two parts of the peninsula and be able to start your walk in no time. As impressive a structure as it is, however, this bridge does feel a little out of kilter with the rugged terrain, and you won't be surprised to learn it's a fairly new addition. As recently as 1984, people wishing to cross – including the local farmers who wanted to take their cattle down from the north to the market – needed to take a small ferry. It wasn't a long trip by all accounts, but the traffic delays it caused meant that frequently it could take hours to traverse the western

Glencoul bothy

coast here in the northwest. Now the only boats you'll find here, other than those of the local fishermen, are pleasure craft. Given this history, it seems apt to combine not just a couple of bothies into a true wilderness weekend, but also add a way back on one such vessel so that you can admire the terrain you've just conquered while resting your tired legs.

The distance doesn't look too demanding, especially on a 1:50,000 OS map, where a friendly path is marked on the ground. And when you start your journey from the rough car park just north of the centre of the hamlet, probably watching one of the many local grey or common seals (the latter having a dog-like face; the former more of a longer, Roman nose) popping up to sneak a peek at you, you'll once again write this off as an easy traverse. But don't be fooled: this route will keep you on your toes. One minute, it'll feel like a pleasant country stroll; the next, you'll be confronted by an alarming sheer drop to the water. Just as you're admiring the views from a path of rocks so neat you'd swear they were flagstones, the terrain breaks up and you have to drag your attention back to the task at hand. You'll be longing for the curve of the loch to reveal itself, dreaming about reaching that first bothy at Glendhu and just about to give up hope, when suddenly it will appear so easily that you'll wonder what you've been worrying about.

This first bothy is part of the still very active Glendhu estate and due to the high population of both red and roe deer – which you may well

Looking out over Loch Glendhu from Kylestrome

encounter on your walk – it's not uncommon to see shooting parties setting out. From August to October, therefore, you should call ahead to make sure there's no stalking taking place while you plan to walk. Once you get to Glendhu bothy, you'll find plenty of rooms and a stove, making it a great, warm first night.

Getting to the next bothy at Glencoul – a former residence built by the Duke of Westminster in the 1880s for estate keepers – is also a wilder and more demanding walk than the map may suggest. In good weather, the views you get from the mere 205m highest point *en route* are a fine reward and Loch Glencoul itself will really take your breath away. This area forms part of a Global Geopark and boasts a varied geology – from quartzite to mylonite – that will impress geologists. For those of us more interested in a rest, the first glimpse of the bothy will inspire similar excitement. But don't get complacent: you still have to overcome a potentially problematic river crossing, as the footbridge was recently washed away. Make sure you take a tent in case it's too dangerous to ford. Once over the river and finally at the stone shelter, the relief and sense of achievement will be overwhelming. And when the boat comes to collect you the following day, you can smugly point out to your fellow passengers (usually day-trippers, come to see the waterfall) the route you took, and realise that – even by water – it's still a fair old distance. Congratulate yourself on a job well done: an unforgettable three-day adventure.

HERE'S THE PLAN
DAY 1

1 Leave the car park at Kylestrome and turn right to head downhill. At the bottom, where the road you're walking on bends to the right, leave it and take the path to your left.

2 Follow this path as it takes you along the water's edge. The path is wide but rough and easy to follow. Look out for seals in the water.

3 At the power plant keep to the lower path. Cross the bridge and continue above the shores of Loch Gleann Dubh as the path becomes rockier underfoot. Continue east and you'll soon spy the buildings of the Glendhu estate. The bothy is the first one you'll come to. It's a big structure, offering two large rooms downstairs and two upstairs.

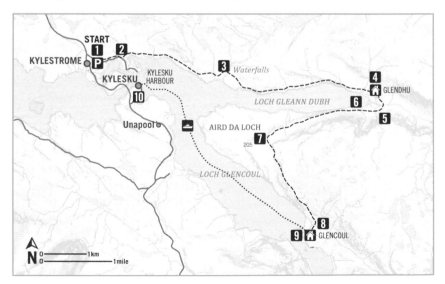

Common seal (Mike Unwin)

TOP Leaving the hamlet of Kylestrome for Glendhu bothy
BOTTOM Entrance to Glendhu bothy

DAY 2

4 Before you leave, it's well worth taking the time to look at the headland opposite you to make out the route of the path – especially as the first bit can be faint. Then turn left from the bothy to continue to the head of the loch. A footbridge will take you safely over the river.

5 Here the path becomes fainter. Don't panic: you'll pick it up again (near the large boulders close to the water's edge). For now, make your way west. It's tempting to keep close to the loch as it's flatter, but beware: the rocks here are extremely slippery with algae and seaweed. Note the small streams you'll cross, then about 100m later you'll pick up the path again – heading west, diagonally uphill.

6 You'll start gaining height fairly quickly over rocks on a very narrow path. This route can become a stream in heavy rain. Eventually it will reach something of a summit at 205m.

7 At this point it can get a little confusing. Ignore the numerous deer tracks that cut temptingly downhill. Your path begins to rise a little here, heading first east then southeast around the rock promontories above. It may feel at one point as though you're heading for the summit but don't worry: just as this happens you will begin to descend again, all the while enjoying the views down to Loch Glencoul – and soon the bothy, too. Here the two waterfalls can cause small landslips, so do take care crossing them. Eventually you'll cut downhill and join the main path that bears southeast.

> **TOP TIP** Know your river crossings. Look for a shallow and — most important — slow-moving section of the river. Make sure you have good walking poles. While crossing, face upstream and keep your pole upstream of you so that the current forces it into the streambed. Keep two contact points on the ground at all times — if you lift your pole, keep both legs still and move only one foot at a time. Do not be afraid to turn back. Never cross a river in spate.

8 Turn right onto this path and look for a safe place to cross the river. The footbridge shown on the OS map was washed away in the summer of 2014, so you must be prepared to ford it (see *Top Tip*). If the river is in spate, do not attempt this. Instead pitch your tent here and enjoy a night in this beautifully wild place. If the river is safe to cross, then do so and make the short few steps past the barn and outbuildings up to Glencoul bothy. This is a small, two-roomed affair (don't be fooled by the locked house behind it). If you've still got some energy, it's well worth walking up the small hillock in front to check out the memorial, and for the great views of your night's shelter and the loch.

DAY 3

9 Wake up, enjoy the view and wait for your boat to arrive to take you back to the harbour.

10 From the harbour, head uphill, turn right and follow the road (carefully) back to the turn-off at Kylestrome. Turn right here and back to your car.

⅄ Drying out kit inside Glencoul bothy

NUTS & BOLTS

PRE-TRIP Kylesku has only one hotel option, so do book ahead if you want accommodation near the start. Otherwise Ullapool is a good alternative before and after your escapade, with a range of B&Bs, hotels and even a hostel. There's also a supermarket, a good camping supply shop and a bookshop that's well stocked with maps and local guidebooks.

PUBLIC TRANSPORT Local bus 891 (North West Community Bus; 🖱 www. transportdirect.info) runs most days from Dingwall (via Ullapool) to Kinlochbervie, with a stop at Kylesku. It takes a couple of hours.

WHEN TO GO Due to potentially hazardous river crossings at other times, this route is best in summer. Late spring or early autumn (providing the weather has been good for a couple of weeks before your visit) may also be an option. Don't worry about crowds: this is quite an undiscovered area. Midges and ticks are a reality – wear repellent and check yourself at the end of each day.

IF YOU DON'T FANCY THE BOTHY? Take your tent, and you'll have the choice of many a good wild camp spot.

SHORT OF TIME? For a quick and easy adventure, there's no shame in forgetting the boat and just doing the walk into Glendhu bothy. This walk is varied and long enough to give you a flavour of the area and you'll still have the chance to spot seals, deer and birdlife on your way. The bothy is big too, meaning you have more chance of a room to yourself.

TIME TO SPARE? If the weather has been good, meaning rivers are OK to cross, then it's worth sticking around to explore this true pocket of wilderness. Be sure to take a stroll up to see Eas a' Chual Aluinn before you leave: this is the highest waterfall in Britain, and three-times higher than Niagara. You could also wild camp by one of the lochs a few kilometres up from the bothy. The really hardy may try to return to the start without the boat by heading south past Loch an Eircill to pick up a path heading northwest back to the A894, but the going will be very hard and navigation difficult, so this one is only for the experienced.

MORE INFO
Up-to-date bothy conditions 🖱 www.mountainbothies.org.uk
Boat schedules and booking 🖱 www.rachaelclare.com
Kylesku 🖱 www.visitscotland.co.uk
Geopark 🖱 www.nwhgeopark.com
NB: Stalking season runs 12 Aug– 20 Oct: call ahead if walking during this time
(☎ 01971 502220)

Eas a' Chual Aluinn Waterfall (Paul Sammonds) ➤

23 HOPE SPRINGS ETERNAL

**STAY UP ALL NIGHT TO WITNESS
THE SUMMER SOLSTICE FROM SCOTLAND'S
MOST NORTHERLY MUNRO, BEN HOPE, SUTHERLAND**

WHERE	Ben Hope, Sutherland
DURATION	1 night, 2 days
START/FINISH	Ben Hope car park ♥ NC461476
MAPS	Landranger (1:50,000) 9; OS Explorer (1:25,000) 447

There's something magical about the summer solstice: 21 June, the one day of the year when the sun is in the sky for more minutes than on any other day. Pagans love it. You've probably seen it on the news: crowds of modern-day Wiccans – and, let's be honest, festival-lovers – descending on Stonehenge to watch the sun rise and set over the ancient stones. But up in Scotland there is an even better way to mark this event.

Ben Hope may sound like the name of a positive thinker or friendly local but it is, in fact, a hill. And not just any hill: this is the most northerly Munro in Scotland; the final high point before the sea swallows the last of the land. Indeed, if you were able to walk on water and decided to head due north from the trig point on its lonely top, you would not reach solid land again until – following a tantalising glimpse of the Orkneys to the east and the Faroes to your west, and passing over the frozen waters of the Arctic – you landed on the shore of Siberian Russia. Yes, Ben Hope is a true outpost. And, as such, it enjoys something of a legendary status

> **NOT JUST ANY HILL: THIS IS THE MOST NORTHERLY MUNRO IN SCOTLAND**

among outdoor folk. Some claim that on the summer solstice, due to the mountain's northerly co-ordinates and its looming height of 927m, you can watch the sun sink behind the horizon then barely set before it starts to rise again. Imagine that! A virtual midnight sun right here in the UK.

But does it actually happen? Well, yes and no. Unfortunately, as the solstice happens on just one day each year, the chances that it will be sunny on that day (and this is Scotland, remember) are slim, to say the least. I've tried it three times and each time been thwarted by the weather. But that's what's so great about those of us who love adventure: we never stop trying.

The ultimate goal would be to climb to the top of Ben Hope towards the end of the day, in no particular hurry, then set up camp somewhere near the fairly flat (though rocky) summit in order to watch the fabled light show. I'll warn you now, though: the walk up from Streathmore feels longer than the kilometres on the map suggest, particularly in bad weather, and I've seen many abandon summit attempts and pitch in the lay-by – no bad idea, given that this is still a very quiet, remote setting. There are certainly a number of flatter sections *en route* that offer further alternatives should the need arise. Indeed, one at the white water of Allt na Caillich, just before the rib of rock at Creag Riabhach, where the climb plateaus onto some boggy ground before pulling up to the summit, has a stream right outside your tent. This is a good plan B – and, over the years, has for me become something of a plan A.

Given that the odds are well and truly against you on this quest, I've often been intrigued – as I'm sure you will be – by the reason for the mountain's optimistic name. It's not, as you might think, to do with the hope inspired by reaching the hard-won summit, nor that its reassuring bulk might have fired up our deity-believing ancestors. Neither is it some ironic name – a cruel joke for hopeful walkers, driven, like me, to despair by yet again failing to see the sunset. In fact, the name derives from the Gaelic word 'hop', which once meant 'bay', owing to the mountain's position between nearby Loch Eriboll and the Kyle of Tongue.

No need to dwell on the negative, though. You may be one of the lucky ones, your efforts rewarded with views over the Pentland Firth and beyond. You might also glimpse some red deer, or even one of the local ospreys wheeling overhead. No matter what your approach, enjoy your summer solstice on this great mountain. And whatever happens, don't lose Hope.

HERE'S THE PLAN
DAY 1

1 Leaving the car park, follow the path signposted 'Way Up Ben Hope', which cuts vaguely north. Follow it uphill, fairly steeply at first, winding alongside the photogenic Allt a' Mhuiseil waterfall. It's then quite a pull until you reach a flatter section, where the path begins to cut more to the west.

2 Though not marked on any of the OS maps, the path is clear on the ground at this point. From this height you will already begin to see the valley open up behind you, with the snaking river of Strathmore now a wide silver serpent on the landscape below. Another pull will take you to just above the 400m contour line, from where you will begin the slow, steady climb to the summit.

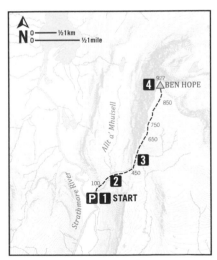

3 Before turning uphill, look to your east. Just above the point where the two rivers converge, just below the 500m mark, is a good, sheltered spot to tuck in your tent or bivvy should a summit sleep be out of the question. Once you've mentally prepared yourself – and, if you're lucky, spotted a red deer or two – then it's time to make a bid

A defeated camper pitched at the start of Ben Hope's summit trail
Look out for the local ospreys (Mike Unwin)

for the top. The path meanders up, keeping you a reasonably safe distance from the drops to your west. Keep following it, though it may at times feel like an endless, unchanging conveyor belt, and eventually the grassy ground gives way to rockier terrain. Finally, just when you think you won't ever really reach the top, the splintered stones of the summit come into view and the trig point is yours for the touching. From here, if you're lucky, you can enjoy the views out over the sea and, possibly, watch the sun never quite set below the waves as the night ticks on. Pitching your tent will be tricky, as there are a lot of rocks, but with some creative thinking a bivvy will tuck in nicely. Plus you're here to watch the sky, so who really wants to sleep through it anyway?

DAY 2

4 Hopefully (pun definitely intended), you've been lucky enough to watch the endless light show. Now, triumphantly, retrace your steps all the way from the summit back to the start.

TOP TIP Make sure you have a good, sturdy sleeping mat as, if you're not careful, the rocky summit can make mincemeat of any super lightweight models. Tarp or a survival bag can be used for this.

208

NUTS AND BOLTS

PRE-TRIP Driving this far north takes a while (depending on where you're coming from) so to make it in time for the Solstice it's best to arrive the day before. If you're feeling adventurous, a great option would be to combine this sleep with the night on Sandwood Bay (page 228). The two are near enough that you could make a perfect weekend of it. If you simply want to come up early and stay in some more traditional accommodation, then try Durness or Tongue, where you can also pick up pre-trip supplies.

PUBLIC TRANSPORT Very infrequent and difficult. The nearest you can get to this route by bus is Eriboll. Take the thrice-daily Nicholas Hird line 802 from Durness. But it's still far from there. Coming from Tongue, try Transport for Tongue (transportfortongue. co.uk).

WHEN TO GO If you're coming to check out the Winter Solstice then it has to be 21 June. You certainly don't have to limit yourself though: any time in summer would command excellent views (as would spring or early autumn). Keep an eye on the weather, and if it's cloud-free and clear on one of the days just before or after 21 June then it's certainly worth doing that instead. And if you do get the views, be sure to send me a photo!

IF YOU DON'T FANCY THE SUMMIT? A good camping spot, much more sheltered, is below the 500m mark on the way up/down to the east of the path. If the weather's awful it's not uncommon for people to put up their tents next to their car, though this is nowhere near as fun.

SHORT OF TIME? If you just want to take in the views from this lofty northern giant there's no harm in nipping up to the summit and back in the daytime and heading home. If you're fit, this should take no more than half a day.

TIME TO SPARE? Take a look around: this far north you're surrounded with options for a great night or two's camping. The immediate choices involve an exploration of the land and lochs north and east of Ben Hope; these offer good water sources and options for pitching. Do note that these areas are mostly pathless and can get extremely boggy, so before setting out ensure you are proficient at navigation, have a good map and compass, and enough supplies.

MORE INFO
Mountain weather www.mwis.org.uk
Local www.discoversutherland.co.uk
Scotland www.visitscotland.com

WHERE	Torridon coast, Wester Ross, Scotland
DURATION	2 nights, 3 days
START/FINISH	Parking lay-by at Lower Diabaig ♥ NG789605
MAPS	OS Landranger (1:50,000) 19; OS Explorer (1:25,000) 433

t's very rare that a road journey rivals the thrill of a wild walking route. But on this drive to the start of a wander along the Torridon coastline, the journey is almost as fun as the destination. Once you turn off the road at Kinlochewe you're plunged into the belly of a mountain wonderland, the single-track road lined by giant upon sandstone giant. You'll have to stop, repeatedly, to let other cars past – particularly in summer. But, unlike on any other road in the British Isles, the drivers here don't look bored out of their wits as they pull over into yet another passing place but are beaming with glee at each new view of the mountains. Except, of course, for the

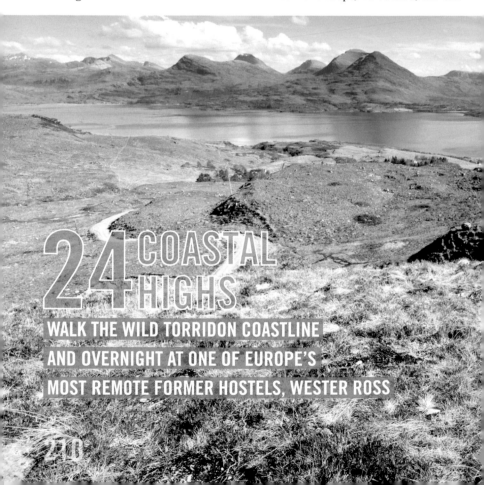

locals, who race past the tourists too busy gawping at their surroundings to even notice them.

Just when you don't think things can get any better you reach Torridon itself, the tiny village that borders the sea loch of the same name. Your route creeps along

> " **ONE OF THE MOST BEAUTIFULLY SITUATED BOTHIES THERE HAS SURELY EVER BEEN** "

beside the water until you swing right and begin to climb to Lower Diabaig. The roads from this point are not only free of motorists but also provide *Top Gear* wannabes with a true roller-coaster of a highway, which winds up and down and round and round, as though built from a mischievous child's crayon squiggle. By the time you reach the truly minuscule hamlet of Lower Diabaig, where this adventure starts, you're already running on adrenaline. And once you pull on your hiking boots it only gets better.

The peaks in this region of Scotland certainly steal much of its glory – and if you've studied geology, you've probably heard the name Torridon before,

Loch Torridon from Bealach Na Gaoithe (Dave Head/S)

211

as this region is home to the well-known Torridonian sandstone, which attracts geology students from all over. But aside from the gneiss and glacial scoops that make up the mountains, the star of the show could just as well be the coastline. Stretching from Diabaig, a crofting and fishing township in the south, to Redpoint, a former fishing stronghold in the north, is a wonderfully wild stretch of rocky headland. To get from one to the other by road would involve such a long and convoluted journey – we're talking well over an hour – that walking between them is actually a perfectly sensible option.

En route, you'll enjoy epic views over to the Outer Hebridean isles of Lewis and Harris and the much nearer Isle of Skye. The abundant birdlife along the coast includes great skuas, divers (red-throated, black-throated and great northern) and, if you're lucky, a white-tailed eagle, and you may spy red deer in the hills. Your first night will involve a beachside camp at the old Redpoint fishing station.

Your second night will be at Craig. This former fishing/crofter's house was taken over by the Scottish Youth Hostels Association (SYHA) back in 1935. It was once legendary throughout Europe as the 'most remote hostel in the UK' – until 2003, when it ceased operation. Thankfully the heroic Mountain Bothies Association took over maintenance in 2006 and now, though you won't get the watchful eye of a warden and luxury of pre-booking a bed before you arrive, you will find an outside 'proper' toilet, and – if you arrive early enough – potentially a bed frame and proper mattress. It may no longer boast the accolade of 'most remote hostel', but you will still get to stay in one of the most beautifully situated bothies there has surely ever been.

Reaching Lochan Dubh ⋀

HERE'S THE PLAN
DAY 1

1 Leave your car in a sensible position within the lay-by, not blocking the road or the driveway to the farm at the top. Then cross the road and pass through the gate in the fence, following the sign pointing to 'Gairloch via Craig'. There's then a deer fence with another gate to take you through.

2 From here, the path takes you around the headland while steadily gaining height. It can be boggy in places and crosses several streams, though there are stepping stones that even after heavy rain should still remain passable. Views out to sea and the island of Sgeir Dughaill will begin to appear to your left as you climb. After the third stream, with high rocky walls on either side, you'll emerge onto more level ground, the trail punctuated with rocky slabs between the stones. It's easy here to take one of several paths made by walkers. As long as you keep tracking roughly north this won't be a problem.

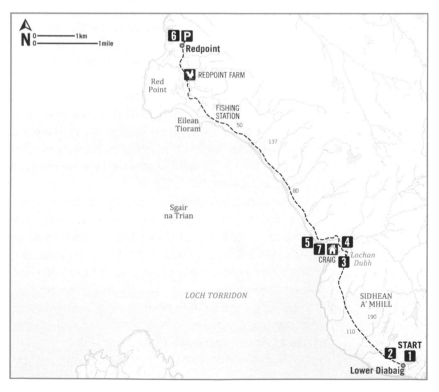

3 When you come to Lochan Dubh you'll notice the wind can really pick up as you're on something of a high point. The path skirts around this small patch of water, bearing slightly northeast, before swinging back around the rocks and beginning the descent to Craig. You'll spot this former SYHA hostel almost immediately as you follow the path down to the small copse.

4 This will be your accommodation for tomorrow tonight (unless you're doing a truncated route or the weather deteriorates), but it's a good place to pop in for a spot of lunch. Once you're ready to leave, turn right from the bothy to continue on the trail. You'll soon reach a bridge, which you cross, and then turn left to follow the Craig River down towards the sea. Before you reach the beach the path turns right to follow the coastline.

5 The going is tough for most of the way to Redpoint, with a less well-used track than the one from Lower Diabaig, and may take longer than you've imagined. But persevere over the grass, rocks and slabs and eventually you'll emerge beside the ruined fishing stations at Redpoint.

TOP TIP The easiest way to collect water from the river by Craig bothy is to head along the path towards the bridge (as though going to Redpoint) and then turn right before you reach it. Carefully cut down the bank to find a flattened section beside the water from where you can safely collect as much as you need.

Eilean Tioram at Redpoint beach (Mike Unwin)

There's plenty of options for a wild camp here: you could pitch near the buildings for shelter; among the grassy hollows between the sand dunes; or trek up to Red Point headland and find a spot there. If it's a calm weather forecast, and you've checked the tides, you could also walk across the causeway of stones to Eilean Tioram – a small rocky islet projecting from Redpoint Beach – and perch there for a while to watch the sunset. It's a magnificent beach to have to yourself, and not an experience you'll forget in a while.

DAY 2

6 After waking in your beachside idyll it's time to retrace your steps from yesterday. Follow the path back along the coast bearing southeast, turning inland only when you reach the Craig River to get to the bridge, where you can cross to continue back to Craig bothy. While here, nip down to take a look at the beach: not only is there a lovely strip of sand but the old ruined homesteads are also worth an exploration. You'll be pleased to know that Craig comes with its own outside toilet: a true treat in the wilderness.

DAY 3

7 Ensure you leave the bothy in a better condition than you found it. Then, as though you were never there, leave this wonderfully wild place and retrace your steps to the start.

LEFT Best bedroom ever at Craig bothy
RIGHT Signpost to Redpoint; Craig bothy

NUTS AND BOLTS

PRE-TRIP Getting to Torridon can be something of an epic journey, but it is well worth it. While there, before heading to Lower Diabaig, it's nice to spend time in Torridon itself. There's a fantastic free campsite near the visitors' centre, not to mention a selection of eateries and a general store to pick up supplies.

PUBLIC TRANSPORT Reaching the start of the walk by bus is, sadly, impossible. The nearest you can get is Torridon, on the once-daily 705 Westerbus from Kinlochewe. From there, your only option for the remaining 20km+ is a taxi.

WHEN TO GO The walk along the Torridon coast is spectacular, no matter what time of the year. In winter the ground is crisp and frozen, and the winter-coated mountains are a sight to behold. In autumn, you may catch sight of the local red deer trying to blend into the rich golden hues of the season. In spring and summer, the longer nights and big skies make this stretch of coastline not just a pleasure to walk but also to linger.

IF YOU DON'T FANCY THE BOTHY? There's no shortage of spots perfect for pitching a tent along the way, and also at the beach near the bothy.

SHORT OF TIME? You could simply walk in and out to see the bothy and beach, though a stay is highly recommended — as is a visit to Redpoint.

TIME TO SPARE? Torridon is a truly special part of the Wester Ross region and worth sticking around to explore further. Whether just spending time lochside in the village, staring up at the mountains from below or pulling on your hiking boots to get to grips with Beinn Alligin, Liathach and Beinn Eighe, there's enough wild landscape to keep you busy for days.

MORE INFO
Up-to-date bothy conditions ☗ www.mountainbothies.org.uk
Torridon Coast ☗ www.discovertorridon.co.uk
Scotland ☗ www.visitscotland.com

Torridon Mountains and Upper Loch Torridon from the southern shore (Dave Head/S)

WHERE	Fisherfield Forest, Wester Ross, Scotland
DURATION	2 nights, 3 days
START	Kinlochewe ⚲ NH029619
FINISH	Dundonnell ⚲ NH092879
MAPS	OS Landranger (1:50,000) 19; OS Explorer (1:25,000) 433, 435; Harvey Superwalker (1:25,000) An Teallach and Fisherfield

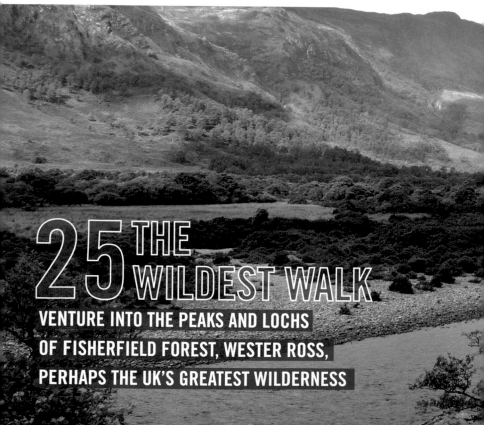

Scotland is big. Very big. I mean, there are times when even I think the walk from the pub to the taxi rank is long, but that's nothing compared with the Highlands. And as anyone down south knows, a drive up to Scotland is a proper drive. But there are places it takes as long to reach from Edinburgh as it takes to reach Edinburgh from London (especially if you get stuck behind a caravan, which you will do). And, even more impressive, there are parts of it that you can only get to on foot.

Fisherfield is a prime example. This remote tract of glacially scoured peaks and glens defines the term 'wild'. It's home to the 'most remote

25 THE WILDEST WALK

VENTURE INTO THE PEAKS AND LOCHS OF FISHERFIELD FOREST, WESTER ROSS, PERHAPS THE UK'S GREATEST WILDERNESS

Munro' (a mountain over 3,000ft) in the country, meaning it's the most distant hill of any great size from any road. To walk across the area takes a minimum of three days (maybe two, if you rush it), and will tax both your navigation and your knees. But the feeling you get when you've completed your mission is hard to describe. You'll take a look at a map and see that you've covered a mammoth distance, and be able to brag of having crossed a truly Great Wilderness.

> **THIS REMOTE TRACT OF GLACIALLY SCOURED PEAKS AND GLENS DEFINES THE TERM 'WILD'**

Discovering the epic size of this jaw-dropping landscape is best done via a network of bothies. For those who have never tried it, bothying can sound a rather bizarre notion: the idea that you can sleep for free in a rudimentary house in the middle of the mountains seems almost too good to be true. But it's something that's been going on since the end of World War II, when mountaineering increased in popularity and hill

Above Loch Maree

219

farming declined, leaving buildings abandoned and deteriorating. Thanks to the Mountain Bothies Association (MBA), over 100 of these shelters (in Scotland, northern England and Wales) are now lovingly maintained by volunteers, making staying tent-free out in the mountains a much easier prospect.

This adventure takes in two such bothies: one on the private estate of Carnmore; the other called Shenavall, which is in the care of the MBA. Both are very basic: see them as stone tents rather than anything else. For a bathroom they provide a shovel – and you will need to use it. But the great thing is that these shelters will protect you from the swarms of midges common in the northern Highlands, not to mention allowing you the space to stretch out and get dressed and, of course, a great place to dry off should you (and your kit) need it.

As well as staying in one of the most ruggedly beautiful places in the UK, you'll get to experience a much simpler way of overnighting in the wilds, and will leave wondering why you ever needed all your mod cons. The journey takes you through some fascinating geology: a sandwich of metamorphic bedrock, sedimentary filling and sparkling quartzite for seasoning – and all exposed by erosion in various forms, from crumbling

TOP Pine martens inhabit the woodland around Loch Maree (Mark Sisson/FLPA) 🔺
BOTTOM Inside Carnmore

pinnacles to towering buttresses and rock-scattered gullies. The name 'forest' is misleading: you won't see many trees for much of the route. You should, however, come across red deer, even if they scarper before you get a decent view, and you might – if you keep scanning the ridges – glimpse a golden eagle. Pine martens also frequent the woodland around Loch Maree, where the rare black-throated diver has one of its most important UK breeding sites. During summer you may spot a feast of wild flowers at your feet, from Arctic mouse-ear and fragrant bog myrtle to alpine lady's mantle and the unmistakeable fluffy tops of cotton grass.

My greatest memory of this adventure was sitting outside Shenavall on my last night (I'd stretched the journey out to four days). The sun set a burning shade of pink, bathing the mountains opposite in a red haze. There was no-one else around for miles, no sound from roads or lights from houses, just me and the bothy. Bliss.

HERE'S THE PLAN
DAY 1

1 Head east from Kinlochewe, crossing the river at the bridge and passing through the collection of houses at the easternmost end. Follow the obvious path around the farmer's field, up and behind the buildings, until you join the track.

2 Follow this path, now heading firmly northwest. This is your longest, straightest stretch. In some areas it will be very faint and in others almost entirely hidden by towering bracken. All the way, though, Loch Maree will remain on your left and the mountain range that includes Slioch will be on your right.

3 After about 10km you will reach the sudden grandeur of the Letterewe estate. Here the path skirts the buildings to the right and begins to climb uphill. Follow it

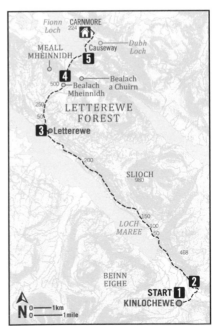

until you top out on Bealach Mhèinnidh, a col between two peaks. Opening up before you will be the kind of views you would expect to greet a hero at the end of a Hollywood movie: sun-drenched Fionn Loch sparkling below, its neighbour Dubh Loch appearing as a distorted reflection mirrored to the southeast. The rocky cathedrals of Carn Mòr and Sgùrr na Laocainn loom like giants above the lochs.

4 Follow the path downhill, between the guard-like peaks of Meall Mhèinnidh and Beinn Lair, passing through their craggy gateway into what must be one of the most wild and beautiful places in the world: an amphitheatre of rugged peaks bursting through the grassy emerald carpet in every direction.

5 You'll eventually reach the valley floor and the sandy shoreline of the loch. Turn right, heading west until you reach the gravelly causeway that divides the water into two lochs. Cross this, and at the buildings of the Carnmore estate you'll see a sign advising climbers and walkers that they can sleep in the barn. This is your bed for the night.

DAY 2

6 Leave the barn and climb alongside Allt Bruthach an Easain, heading steadily uphill. The path cuts up the hillside, depositing you much higher into the mountains at Fuar Loch Mòr. Here it forks.

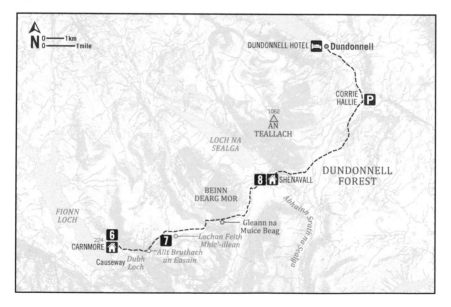

⬥ **TOP** Looking over to the rugged buttress of Slioch (David Head/D)
BOTTOM Carnmore barn awaits walkers; Above Loch Maree *en route* to the bothy

TOP TIP Bothies in this area can be full, especially when the weather is good, as these mountains form part of a round called the Fisherfield Six. It's worth packing a bivvy bag or tent, just in case.

Peering down into Fisherfield ⋀

7 Unless you have extra time in which to head south and explore more mountains and wild camp opportunities, take the east fork towards the spiky giant of An Teallach (another great mountain to explore on a day with more time). The route ahead can get a little boggy but, surrounded by the most majestic mountains this part of Scotland has to offer, you won't really care. Persevere, following Gleann na Muice Beag, and you will eventually reach the stream of Gleann na Muice. Follow this north. If it's safe to do so, cross the river onto its east side as soon as you can. Continue north, where another big stream-crossing is in order on Abhainn Srath na Sealga. Once across to the north side of the water you will see the welcome sight of Shenavall bothy.

DAY 3

8 From Shenavall, take the path uphill that runs behind the building, bearing east. It can be very faint in places – and muddy, particularly after heavy rain – but persevere and you will eventually join a wider, more definite forestry track. Follow this, first through open mountains then trees, and you will eventually emerge at the lay-by of Corrie Hallie, a 3km walk from Dundonnell and a celebratory pint.

⛰ Shenavall bothy at sunset

NUTS AND BOLTS

PRE-TRIP If you arrive the night before you start (recommended) there's a great bunkhouse at the Kinlochewe Hotel (☎ 01445-760253; 🖰 www.kinlochewehotel.co.uk) and a small general store down the road to pick up last-minute supplies – ie: camping gas, blister plasters, food. If you do the route in reverse, a good place to stay is the hostel in Dundonnell (☎ 01854 633224; 🖰 www.sailmhor.co.uk). This is self-catering, and there is no general store, so you might decide to sample the An Teallach ale and pub grub nearby at the Dundonnell Hotel.

PUBLIC TRANSPORT The local Westerbus line 700 runs from Inverness to Kinlochewe (five times a week; about 2 hours). You can then pick up the same line 700 bus from Dundonnell back to Inverness (four times a week; under 2 hours). To get back to Kinlochewe from Dundonnell, you'll need to take the local 700 or 707 to Gairloch (six times a week), from where you can catch the 700, 705 or 711 (twice daily) to Kinlochewe.

If driving, two cars are best to complete the mission, leaving one at the start and one at the finish. Otherwise, if you don't want to wait for public transport, you could leave your car at the finish point and organise in advance for the local taxi service (Hy-Jack Taxi Service; ☎ 01445 712452) to take you from there back to your start. It's always easier to end at your car, rather than have to time your return to coincide with a booked taxi.

WHEN TO GO Late spring or summer and autumn are best – in order to avoid midges and crowds. After heavy rain, the two rivers may be impassable, preventing you from reaching Shenavall. Use your judgement: if the water is too high and fast-flowing, turn back and return the way you came – the route will always be here for another (better) day. Snow can make the route very difficult in winter and even well into spring, especially on the high mountain passes. If venturing into Fisherfield in snow, make sure you have appropriate equipment (ie: ice axe and crampons).

IF YOU DON'T FANCY THE BOTHY? Wild camping is a great option on this route. With so much fresh water the mountainous hinterland really is your oyster.

SHORT OF TIME? You could shorten this route by walking to one bothy (either Carnmore or Shenavall), staying one night, then retracing your steps to your start via the way you came in. Or shorten your walk-in: an alternative start point at Poolewe offers a quicker way in to Carnmore, allowing you to walk out from Carnmore to Dundonnell in a single (though extremely long) day.

TIME TO SPARE? When it comes to wild camp options you're spoilt for choice. You could try your hand on Slioch, perhaps summit the mighty An Teallach (the usual route involves a Grade 2 scramble) or head east, where there are other bothies in the area.

MORE INFO

Up-to-date bothy conditions 📷 www.mountainbothies.org.uk

Local 📷 www.kinlochewe.com; www.dundonnell.camusnagaul.com

Walking routes 📖 *Great Mountain Days in Scotland* by Dan Bailey, Cicerone

WHERE	Sutherland, Scotland
DURATION	1 night, 2 days
START/FINISH	Kinlochbervie ⚲ NC195600
MAPS	OS Landranger (1:50,000) 9; OS Explorer (1:25,000) 446

Scotland's far north should feel like a busy place. From the jumping-off point for many a charity challenge across Britain, to where the Vikings used to turn around their giant longboats and head back to Norway, it's seen its fair share of traffic. Yet this rugged 'west end' is a far cry from the tourist trap that is John O'Groats in the east (which is not the most northernmost point of the country, even though it takes all the glory). The site of the famous Cape Wrath lighthouse, with its hardy resident family who stay year-round despite being cut off from the mainland in winter, it has a true end-of-the-earth feel, with no need for comedy signposts or tourist shops selling tartan sticks of rock.

26 SECRET SANDS

SLEEP AMID THE MACHAIR ON THE UK'S MOST SECLUDED BEACH, AT SANDWOOD BAY, SUTHERLAND

What's more, along the shoreline of this remote region lies one of the most remote beaches in mainland Britain. Sandwood Bay comes complete with a good couple of kilometres of golden sand, plus mattress-soft dunes and towering granite cliffs that seem sculpted by some giant artist. Anywhere else in the UK and there'd be a giant car park, deck-chair kiosks and donkey rides quicker than you could say 'promenade'. Sandwood, however, is so remote that it remains perfectly unspoilt.

> " THE SOUND OF CRASHING WAVES WILL LEAD YOU DOWN TO EXPLORE THE SHORELINE "

Even if you're in Scotland already, getting there still takes some effort. You drive north from Glasgow, then further north still, then north some more after that, and – just when you think you're about to run out of land – you turn west and follow the single-track road through tiny hamlets with alluring names: Kinlochbervie, Oldshoremore, Oldshore Beg and Blairmore. Just beyond the last of these, you reach a small, unassuming car

Sandwood Bay at low tide (John A Cameron/S)

park, complete with clean toilets, a freshwater tap and helpful information about the area.

Across from these simple facilities, without fanfare, is the sign that simply states 'Sandwood'. And this is where the fun really begins. The track is fairly clear all the way, but it's rough, rocky and boggy for most of its 5km. Crossing loch edges, battling often strong, chilling wind and climbing a little more steeply than you might think from the map, you finally arrive at this perfect slice of wild.

Clues that the beach is close start to appear before you arrive: first, the crumbling ruins of a former lodge; then a glimpse of Sandwood Loch – so large you'll swear it must be the ocean; next, the cliffs beyond, which enclose this heavenly beach. And then finally, when you see the sand itself, you may well be overcome by the urge to run – as I did, on my first visit.

Curious sheep will follow you about as you pitch your tent among the dunes. Then the sound of crashing waves will lead you down to explore the shoreline. Below the stone stack of Am Buchaille, Celtic for 'The Herdsman', you'll watch as the water powers towards you, breaking over the rocks in the shallows. Gulls will call from overhead as you stare out to sea and picture the Viking ships that would have sailed past these shores over 1,000 years ago.

The John Muir Trust manages and watches over this beach, which is designated a Special Area of Conservation. This status is due mainly to its rare habitat. Sandwood and the surrounding area protects a vital stretch of machair, a low-lying, coastal grassland that grows on a bed of tiny shell fragments and is found only in northwest Scotland and Ireland. Machair supports a rich array of plantlife, including eight different types of orchid, plus breeding wading birds such as dunlins. Around 300 years ago you might still have seen wolves roaming this landscape. Today, keep your eyes peeled instead for red and roe deer inland, and seabirds – including puffins, razorbills and guillemots – out at sea or buzzing around the cliffs.

As sunset tints the sky with pink and orange you'll start to make out the beam from Cape Wrath lighthouse several kilometres away. Then you'll settle in for the night as – far from the nearest light pollution – stars begin to pinprick the darkening sky. Snuggle into your tent or bivvy bag, light up the stove for a hot drink and be lulled asleep by the waves. Perfection.

Arctic terns dive for fish offshore (Mike Unwin)

HERE'S THE PLAN
DAY 1

1 From the John Muir Trust car park, cross the road and head towards the fence where you'll see the sign for Sandwood. Go through the gate and follow the well-marked trail with Loch Aisir down to your right.

2 You'll know you've reached Loch na Gainimh when it's windy, as the gusts tear across the water with such ferocity you'll think you're already at the sea. You'll notice on the map that a smaller path diverts from the main trail to cut off the corner. In good weather this is an option, as you can pick it out among the grassy hummocks. After a lot of rain, however, or in the dark, it's best to stick to the main path. The obvious left turn is clear when you reach the end of the water. Take it, ignoring the track, which continues straight.

3 Stay on the main path now, ignoring any slight turn-offs as you reach higher ground. You'll come to a gate in a fence, which you pass through. From here on, the path is less of a well-used track and more of a trail beaten into the landscape. Looking at the map you'll notice three main lochs you will pass on your way to the beach. These are useful clues for navigation, especially in bad weather. I like to tick them off in my head to know where I am on the map. First is the larger Loch a' Mhuilinn on your

left, where you skirt very close to the shore and will need to take stepping stones across. Next up is the smaller Loch Meadhonach, and finally Loch Clais nan Coinneal, both on your right.

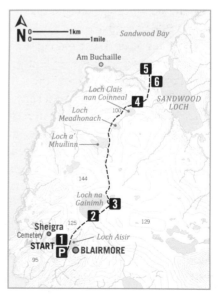

4 Once past the last loch, you'll see that the path begins to descend. You'll now catch your first glimpse of the mammoth Sandwood Loch, which feeds into the ocean, and also spot on the horizon the dilapidated ruin of the former lodge. You may decide to go and explore this first. Otherwise, continue downhill. You will notice the ground becoming increasingly sandy. Sheep abound in

TOP TIP Be careful if exploring the beach to the north side of the tributary that connects Sandwood Loch to the sea. This can deepen, widen and begin flowing very fast as the tide comes in, and you don't want to be cut off from your tent and the safety of the dunes. Be aware of the sea conditions – and where the sea is – at all times.

this area, meaning lots of tracks. But you can't go far wrong: just listen for the sound of waves and continue to descend. Soon you'll emerge onto the sand.

5 You'll notice a few things from your new vantage point. To your left is the sea stack of Am Buchaille, a pinnacle first scaled by two hardy climbers back in 1968 (and not that many since). Directly in front of you is a stack of rocks where, in the early 1900s, a reputable local man and farmer called Alexander Gunn swore he saw a mermaid. This was no Disney-style Little Mermaid, but a fierce creature, seven feet long, with yellow skin, and eyes the same wild green and blue of the sea she was trying to lure him into. Sea creatures aside, you can also watch the terns and other seabirds darting over the water and up to the cliffs that surround you on either side. As darkness falls, you'll begin to spy the beam from the Cape Wrath lighthouse. Pitch your tent amongst the soft grassy dunes, above the tideline; you can easily gather water from the loch behind the beach. Then watch as the sun sinks below the horizon on this picture-perfect beach and stars begin to pinprick the sky above. The place is yours, and yours alone.

DAY 2

6 Gulls will probably be your alarm clock the next morning. After enjoying your breakfast from one of the best views imaginable, pack up your things and simply retrace your steps from the walk-in.

⊲ Looking down over Sandwood Bay

⊼ **TOP** Am Buchaille guards the waves
CENTRE Puffin (Mike Unwin); View from the tent flap
BOTTOM Lighthouse at Cape Wrath (Kevin Fletcher/D)

233

NUTS AND BOLTS

PRE-TRIP As Sandwood is so difficult to get to, you may want to consider staying somewhere nearby before your walk in. The nearest large town for supplies and accommodation options is Ullapool – though that is still around two hours' drive away. Other much nearer options include Kinlochbervie, which offers a couple of hotels, or Durness. If you choose the latter, in summer (mid-April – September) you could take the passenger ferry over the Kyle of Durness (from Kyle of Keodale, two miles south of Durness), either the day before or day after your adventure, to visit the Cape Wrath lighthouse. From there it's an 11-mile walk or a mini bus ride (offered by the lighthouse owners) where you can visit the building and meet the hardy people who live there year-round. Check ferry times in advance: the MOD use the land around Cape Wrath so you need to make sure access is not restricted when you want to visit (NB: this won't affect a visit to Sandwood Bay via Blairmore).

PUBLIC TRANSPORT Long and very infrequent, but possible to get close. The nearest bus stop is in Kinlochbervie (about 8km from the start). This is either a 4.5-hour bus ride from Inverness (bus 804) or you could take the train from Inverness to Wick, getting off at Lairg (1hr 40mins), then take bus 806 to Durness and get off at Kinlochbervie. Other bus options are available from Ullapool.

WHEN TO GO Sandwood Bay is a superb spot all year. In winter the moody skies and big waves make it an exciting outpost, in summer the calm, blue waters can trick you into thinking you've made it to the Caribbean – and you may find yourself sharing the beach with the odd surfer. Spring and autumn bring fewer visitors and fewer midges.

IF YOU DON'T FANCY THE BEACH? Some people are nervous about pitching on sand, especially if they are not confident about how far in the tide will come. If that's you, then you can always perch your tent higher up near the abandoned lodge, where it's grassier and definitely in no danger from the sea, or on some of the land before you reach the beach – perhaps near to a loch for fresh water.

SHORT OF TIME? A day walk into Sandwood Bay is equally rewarding for those not feeling inclined to overnight. Though it may be worth taking a bivvy and supplies in case you change your mind. Well, you have come this far…

TIME TO SPARE? There are plenty of options to explore the area further if you have time, although good navigation skills in all weathers and the ability to read a map and use a compass are vital, as after Sandwood the walking is pathless and rough. One option is to extend your visit to include a stay at Strathchailleach bothy (maintained by the MBA, marked on the OS map). This sits 3km from the beach and involves a scramble up onto the cliffs on the east of the tributary that feeds into Sandwood Loch. It was once the home of a hermit-like character, named James McRory-Smith – aka Sandy, who was reputedly not always welcoming to walkers, but now it's open and welcoming to all. Those are his paintings you'll see on the bothy walls, and you can read more about him and see his picture on the memorial plaque. A stay there will add another dimension to your trip.

MORE INFO
Cape Wrath/ferry to the lighthouse 🐭 www.visitcapewrath.com
John Muir Trust 🐭 www.jmt.org/sandwood-estate.asp
Spooky Sandwood legends 🐭 www.mysteriousbritain.co.uk

Sandwood Bay in glorious sunshine (Peter Chisholm/A)

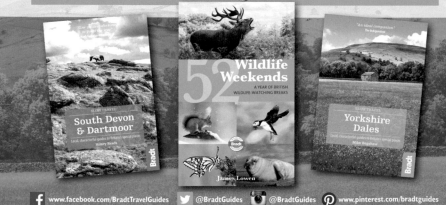

BRITISH CLASSICS SINCE 1965.

We understand you have to make the most of the outside world, you need clothing that will support you. With that in mind we've constructed a range to withstand every environment with an unparalleled appreciation for our traditions, culture and not least our shared sense of identity.

CRAGHOPPERS
World Travel Clothing

40 Years of Pioneering Publishing

In 1974, Hilary Bradt took a road less travelled and published her first travel guide, written whilst floating down the Amazon.

40 years on and a string of awards later, Bradt has a list of 200 titles, including travel literature, Slow Travel guides and wildlife guides. And our pioneering spirit remains as strong as ever – we're happy to say there are still plenty of roads less travelled to explore!

INDEX